"John has consistently raised
nicating world class interview wisdom. His kind, reassuring,
practical advice will help anybody who wants to radically
improve their interview performance and, more than that, to
succeed in the career of their choice."

Sophie Rowan, author of *Brilliant Career Coach* and
Coaching Psychologist at Pinpoint

"John Lees knows his stuff in the careers field and can always
be relied upon to give wise, considered advice. Anybody
thinking about which way to turn in their career would want
somebody like John in their corner."

James Brockett, *People Management Magazine*

"John Lees' approach works because he gives readers simple,
practical steps to help flip their mindsets into the more daring,
exploratory and confident mode needed for career transition
success."

Stuart Lindenfield, Head of Transitions Practice, Reed
Consulting

"John makes you think differently about your career and how
you manage it. He provides really useful and practical tools in
a fun and engaging way."

Gordon McFarland, Head of HR, British Gas Commercial
People Team

The Interview Expert

The
Interview
Expert

Get the job you want

JOHN LEES

PEARSON

Harlow, England • London • New York • Boston • San Francisco • Toronto • Sydney
Auckland • Singapore • Hong Kong • Tokyo • Seoul • Taipei • New Delhi
Cape Town • São Paulo • Mexico City • Madrid • Amsterdam • Munich • Paris • Milan

PEARSON EDUCATION LIMITED

Edinburgh Gate
Harlow CM20 2JE
Tel: +44 (0)1279 623623
Fax: +44 (0)1279 431059
Website: www.pearson.com/uk

First published in Great Britain in 2012

Pearson Education is not responsible for the content of third-party internet sites.

ISBN: 978-0-273-76255-3

British Library Cataloguing-in-Publication Data
A catalogue record for this book is available from the British Library

Library of Congress Cataloging-in-Publication Data
A catalog record for this book is available from the Library of Congress

10 9 8 7 6 5 4 3
17

Designed by Design Deluxe
Typeset in 11pt Sabon by 3
Printed and bound by CPI Group (UK) Ltd, Croydon, CR0 4YY

Contents

Acknowledgements

MY THANKS TO ALL THOSE who have recently updated and challenged my thinking on interviews: Rebecca Alexander (*Psychologies*), Judith Armatage (Recruitment & Employment Confederation), Gill Best (John Lees Associates), Loraine Bones (Say It Works), Claire Coldwell (Ad Astra Career Management), Isabel Chadwick (Career Management Consultants), Deborah Cooper (Warren Partners), Jim Currie (Currie Whiteford), Graeme Dixon (Cast Consulting), Jane Downes (Clearview Coaching Group), Zena Everett (Second Careers), Paula Godley (Godley Associates), Beverley Grant (Verticity), Tony Griffiths (Slade People Solutions), Tim Harney (Springwood Consulting), Shirley Howe (Howe Different), Kate Howlett (Ruspini Consulting), Kathryn Jackson (Career Balance), Karen Kinnear, Stuart McIntosh, Stuart Mitchell (Stuart Mitchell Group), Margaret Middlemiss (FearLess Coaching), Melanie Moore (Farrer Barnes), Bernard Pearce (Career Inspirations), Ann Reynolds, Robin Rose (ACSOL), Sophie Rowan (Pinpoint), Sital Ruparelia (Sital Ruparelia Solutions), Alexandra Sleator (Career Accelerator), Sheryl Spanier (Sheryl Spanier & Company), Joelle Warren (Warren Partners), Fiona Ward (WardLambert HR), Malcolm Watt (Watt Associates), Ruth Winden (Careers Enhanced Ltd), as well as many fellow members of the LinkedIn Career Coach Forum. My particular thanks to Stuart McIntosh for his tough love in scrutinising the first draft, and my wife Jan for her storytelling expertise.

Thanks and appreciation are due to my imaginative and insightful editor Elie Williams at Pearson. Thanks too to my diligent agent James Wills at Watson, Little, and to my very talented publicist Sue Blake.

I'd like to thank Career Management Consultants Ltd (CMC) for the chance to road-test ideas with executive clients. Thanks also to Suchi Mukherjee, MD of Gumtree, and the team at 3 Monkeys, for the opportunity to research employer perspectives.

Finally, one very important and long-due expression of gratitude, and acknowledgement of a debt I can never repay. My work in the careers field began with two summer workshops in Bend, Oregon, where I received over 125 hours of teaching, wisdom and inspiration from Richard Nelson Bolles, author of *What Colour Is Your Parachute?* Thank you, Dick, for your generous spirit.

This book is dedicated to two Andrews, both great chaps: my one and only brother Andrew Lees, and my oldest friend Andrew O'Hanlon.

PUBLISHER'S ACKNOWLEDGEMENTS

We are grateful to McGraw-Hill for permission to reproduce the figure on p. 134. From Lees, John, *Take Control of Your Career* (McGraw-Hill, 2006). Reproduced with kind permission of The McGraw-Hill Companies. All rights reserved.

In some instances we have been unable to trace the owners of copyright material, and we would appreciate any information that would enable us to do so.

About the author

JOHN LEES IS ONE OF THE UK's best-known career strategists. His book *How To Get A Job You'll Love* regularly tops the bestseller lists and has twice been selected as WH Smith's 'Business Book of the Month'. His other titles include *Take Control of Your Career* and *Why You? – CV Messages To Win Jobs*.

As a career and outplacement coach, John has helped people from across the UK to make difficult career decisions

– difficult either because they don't know what to do next, or because there are barriers in the way of success. He is in demand as a keynote speaker at UK events (including *Forum 3*), and has presented at the world's largest international career conferences and at events in the USA, South Africa, Switzerland, Australia and New Zealand.

John is a columnist for *People Management* and regularly appears in the national press and magazines ranging from *Psychologies* to *She*. His work has also been profiled in the *Sunday Times* and *Coaching at Work*. He broadcasts widely on radio and has contributed to the BBC interactive *Back to Work* series programme, BBC 2's *Working Lunch*, Channel 4's *Dispatches* and ITV's *Tonight – How To Get A Job*.

John is a graduate of the universities of Cambridge, London and Liverpool, and has spent most of his career focusing on the world of work. He has trained recruitment specialists since the mid-1980s, and is the former Chief Executive of the Institute of Employment Consultants. He has worked with a large range of organisations, including British Telecom, the British Council, British Gas Commercial, Career Management Consultants Ltd, CIPD, Cranfield School of Management, HBOS, The House of Commons, HSBC, Imperial College, Orange, REC, the Association of MBAs, Lloyds Banking Group, Marks & Spencer, Reuters and Tribal, as well as business schools across the UK. He has been elected as a Career Management Fellow (CMF) by the Institute of Career Certification International and serves on the UK national board of the Association of Career Professionals International.

Alongside his careers work, John serves as an ordained Anglican priest in the Diocese of Chester. He lives and works in Cheshire with his wife, the children's writer, Jan Dean, with occasional visits from their two adult sons.

John Lees Associates provides one-to-one career coaching in most parts of the UK. For details visit **www.johnleescareers.com** or telephone 01565 631625.

Preface

WHY YOU SHOULD READ THIS BOOK

There are plenty of books and websites about job interviews. Most cover the basics well, many reminding you of things you think you already know, but for some reason never get round to putting into practice. Other books make you feel slightly guilty that you couldn't transform yourself into the interview superhero required. You might have been tempted to get instant results by learning textbook answers to interview questions, only to discover they didn't quite match the questions asked, and didn't sound as authentic as you hoped. In any case you struggled to keep all the advice in your head at the same time. The advice sounded useful but didn't seem to address the interview you have tomorrow morning, and didn't get you the job.

This book is designed to take a different approach:

- It looks at the reasons you don't put advice into practice, accepting the fact that you are not going to become the perfect interviewee overnight.

- It takes routine interview advice apart by giving you an insider perspective on what interviewers want.

- It helps you transform your performance, rather than feeling guilty about all the things you could have done.

● It challenges you to look at the small but significant changes you need to make to improve your impact at interview.

● It offers you the wisdom of experienced career coaches, recruiters and HR specialists to answer the questions you would ask if your career coach was in the room.

YOUR 'KILLER APPS'

For those of you who aren't obsessed with the latest technology, the 'killer app' is the bit of software that dominates the market and allows a provider to crush the competition, at least for a few months. You're looking for something similar. Something that differentiates you in a tough market, something that shortens the odds and gives you an edge, but without taking months of preparation or coaching.

The good news is that you don't need to become something you are not. You don't need to be unique, you don't need to be the one candidate in a million, and you *don't* need to fake it. Possessing a killer app just means gaining an edge and being considered a front runner for a post from the moment you walk into the interview room.

What you will discover from this book is that this is only partially about your skills and experience. It is also about your attitude, your impact, and the way you present your evidence at interview. It is about appearing relaxed and in control (even though you won't be). It is about telling good stories rather than spouting pre-rehearsed answers.

THE DIFFICULT NEWS

Although this book is packed with techniques to improve your interview skills and tips to help you get inside the mind of the recruiter, it does not offer you a magic bullet solution. There are things you can do quickly which will improve the odds in your favour and make it more likely that an employer will say 'yes', but you have to do some work. You have to undertake smart research, anticipate questions, and organise your evidence. A job interview is a time management exercise rather like a sports or stage performance – hours of preparation and effort go into a short, heart-stopping burst of activity. Performance under pressure requires time to be put aside in advance – not just preparation of your material, but preparing yourself too, so that you can project the best of yourself in the interview room.

GETTING AN EDGE

Surely everyone can't become an above-average interview candidate? Absolutely right. Despite an abundance of information in books, articles and websites, candidates keep making the same mistakes, either not preparing at all or doing the wrong kind of preparation. Preparation does not just relate to thinking (and worrying) about interviews, but doing the right kind of thinking.

There are people who know how to win interviews on instinct alone (often they are unable to say what it is they do). These are the irritating people who tell you that they get every job they apply for. They sound ultra-lucky, but they have more than luck on their side – they have unconsciously focused their material, behaviours and attitude into the right place at the right time. This book shows you how to consciously apply the same techniques to your performance.

Any one of these chapters will give you an edge and improve your performance. A few hours reading this book will make a difference to the way you see yourself in the interview process, and the results you achieve.

CHAPTER ONE

What makes a great interview performance?

THIS CHAPTER LOOKS AT:

- The behaviours and techniques that get job offers
- Gaining leverage
- Seeing the interview through the eyes of the decision maker
- Job interviews – myths and reality

HOW TO GET IT RIGHT MOST OF THE TIME

Considering the many hundreds of people I meet every year who believe that they don't perform well at interviews, there is clearly a widespread need to achieve some kind of improvement.

You don't need to become the perfect interviewee (and I'm not sure such a person exists – at least I haven't met them yet), but you do need to be completely honest about the areas you could improve. That's an important starting point, because even small changes in your approach will make a difference. So, simply start out by being prepared to make a change.

If you have little experience and you feel very nervous in a job interview, good news – you can make enormous improvements in a short space of time because you don't have interview habits to shake off. If, however, you are a seasoned veteran, you might find it harder to kick the bad habits that have been holding you back. All too often I meet people who have skills in abundance, but they continuously fail at interview. Why? Because they are stuck in one interview 'mode', which they remain in – even when they can see it fails to get the right results.

They nod politely when tips are offered, but their actual strategy is 'I know what I am doing, so leave me alone'. They go into automatic mode in the interview room, putting in the same dull performance, making the same mistakes. Even the most accomplished public speakers refine and tweak what they do and keep themselves open to the possibility that there is at least one thing they could do completely differently. Similarly we all need to keep sharp by keeping an open mind.

The changes you are likely to make are around awareness, mindset and technique: **awareness** of how the interview is experienced by the people in the room making the decisions; rethinking your **mindset** (particularly if you're starting out with 'I don't interview well' running through your head – see Chapter 6 for more about adopting the right thinking before interviews); and, finally, **technique** – the good news is that this can be learned – you don't have to be a natural.

LEVERAGE

If your interviews are not translating into job offers it's easy to believe that you have to change everything – not just what you say, but who you are. That's almost always impossible. You don't have to re-invent yourself. What you do need to do is *change the small things that really matter.* Just altering one or two things (rethinking the way you start an interview, talking about your best skills, or learning good stories) can make the difference between a lacklustre attempt and a star performance, moving you very suddenly from 'no' to a 'definite maybe'.

One of the small things you can do is read this chapter twice – you will find at least one thing here that makes a difference immediately.

WHAT A GREAT PERFORMANCE LOOKS LIKE TO A DECISION MAKER

What do top interviewees do differently? You might think that they pitch themselves aggressively, or they have pre-rehearsed, perfect answers. You might think that they can deliver a three-minute career summary at the drop of a hat. You might think that they are only great at interview because they have great things to talk about. You might feel they are better educated, more articulate, more glamorous than you. Wrong.

This is what managers and HR specialists say about the candidates who brighten up their day:

- Relaxed enough so that they seem themselves and build some kind of relationship in the room.

- Nervous and modest enough to show that the interview is important.

- Careful listeners, focusing on the questions asked.

- Well prepared – they have thought in detail about the organisation and the job. They have prepared material for questions they believe will come up.

- Clearly and genuinely interested in the job as a worthwhile activity, not just as a means of getting a pay cheque.

- Capable of describing their own behaviours, working style and strengths, showing that they have learned from experience.

- Well equipped with a fund of short, memorable examples which showcase their skills and motivation.

- Armed with a small number of very relevant questions.

- On time, on message, and looking and sounding the part from the moment they walk into the building.

Is there anything in this list that you really can't do?

'IT'S AN INTERVIEW, NOT A PERFORMANCE'

I hear this line from people who think an interview is just about content. They couldn't be more wrong. Too many people approach interviews passively – 'I'll just turn up and respond'. This is the perfect strategy for failure. Would you use the same approach for a wedding speech? For an interview to approve your citizenship? For a driving test? For a funding application? There are many occasions when active commitment matters – the way you say what you say, and the evidence you choose to deliver – and a job interview should be close to the top of this list.

An interview is *always* a performance – you have to command your audience's attention, you are on show, everything about you is being observed. An average candidate leaves much of that to chance, or trusts that 'being yourself' wins the day. More effective candidates know that it's the details that tip the balance in their favour.

Let's take another kind of planned performance – a speech. As soon as you stand up the small details are noticed – how you walk up to the lectern, your clothes, hair, glasses, physical confidence – these are all assessed in micro-seconds. The audience then listens intently to your first sentence. If you say 'Is this microphone working?' or 'Sorry, my notes are in the wrong order', your listeners form an immediate conclusion, because that's what we're conditioned to do every time we put our attention onto encountering someone new.

In contrast, if the speaker stands very still, makes eye contact and says 'Thank you for being here today. My name is

Bill, and I want to talk to you about rebuilding this community', the chances are that you decide to buy into the person *and* the message – immediately. The same thing happens in the opening moments of the interview, which is why Chapter 10 tackles the issue head on.

SEEING THE INTERVIEW THROUGH THE EYES OF THE DECISION MAKER

It may sound painfully obvious, yet consistently, and for years, the most common complaints I hear from HR staff, line managers and external recruiters are that candidates:

(a) haven't thought enough about the content of the job;

(b) haven't matched the job to their own experience;

(c) don't package their experience in terms which motivate the recruiter to make a positive decision.

This is the paradox: employers say candidates don't match themselves to the requirements of the job; candidates say this advice is obvious. Both realities co-exist. Perhaps it's because an interview looks deceptively simple, but there is a huge gulf between what interviewers want and what candidates do.

If this is so evident, what does it tell us? That many people *choose* to be under-prepared. They choose not to make obvious, organised connections between what the organisation is looking for and what they have to offer. Why on earth would they do that?

When you're hyping yourself up for a job interview it's easy to forget the perspective of the decision maker. Candidates often fail to appreciate that recruitment is not an inspiring business. Reading CVs, for example, is not something many people look forward to. Although recruiters often talk about enjoying meeting people, interviewing can feel like a chore. So, simply being an interesting candidate will help.

You also need to be more memorable than other candidates. Over 25 years or so I have asked recruiters what impresses them about candidates, and much of their feedback informs this book.

Most of their feedback is about people being people, not about recruitment issues. Interviewers, for example, are more likely to remember you if they like you, or if you share common interests. They are more likely to remember you if you get two or three key messages across. They are more likely to recall you, sadly, if you are the first or the last candidate of the day.

They will also remember you for all the wrong reasons if you immediately make a poor impression, never relax, or say something negative. Beyond that, the dull, average and nondescript is all very quickly forgotten.

Robin Rose, Careers Consultant to Manchester Business School, suggests 'it also helps if you present as someone who is not unlucky. So even if you have been through difficult times, if you say "I was lucky because …" and show how you learned and bounced back, you make a strong impression. Some candidates talk about a long history of business and personal setbacks and just come across as downbeat and unlucky.'

JOB INTERVIEWS – MYTHS AND REALITY

Pushy people get the job	This might be true in roles where assertive behaviour is linked to performance, such as sales jobs, but often the opposite is true.
Interviewees are born, not made	Tell that to all those people who learned the art of being interviewed this year.

You never know what's going to come up in an interview	With the right preparation and mindset you can predict three out of four questions that are going to come up. You'll also have a better chance of answering unexpected questions by spending time getting ready for the unexpected.
No amount of preparation can turn a poor interviewee into a star performer	Applied in the right area, small changes can make a huge difference.
It's a numbers game – you have to attend dozens of pointless interviews	Everything you do to focus your interview skills improves your odds and shortens the race.
You need to learn great answers off by heart	You don't, but you need to have a series of short narratives and know pretty much where each of them is going before you begin.
Interviewers make it up as they go along – it's all unpredictable	Occasionally you will be floored by a curve ball question, but most candidates who say they couldn't understand the questions have just not spent enough time predicting the employer's shopping list.
People lie at interview and get the job	Although candidates commonly over-egg their documentation, at interview it takes a great deal more nerve to lie in the face of probing questions. Don't try it.

▶

If you're quiet and shy you don't do well	Employers are looking for people to do the job, not stand-up comics. Getting your skills evidence across carefully may work – especially if the employer wants someone who will get on with the job quietly.
Without a professional qualification or degree you're always near the bottom of the pile	Many people have successful careers on the strengths of their abilities, know-how and personal characteristics. Learn to show that you can do all the same things that qualification holders do, but you've also got the experience.
Test results count more than interviews	Rarely true. In fact, employers will often adjust or ignore test scores in favour of candidates who 'feel' right.
References give away secret information	Interviewers rarely use references, certainly not in any detail.
The interview is going to check out every detail in my CV	Unlikely. It will focus on areas which clearly match, and those that don't. The interview will almost certainly zoom in on problem areas, such as gaps or incomplete projects – have pre-prepared material for these areas.
Most interviews today are just a formality – the inside track candidate has already got the job	This may be true, and there are sometimes ways of finding out. However, employers are also open to new talent and may even create a new role for you.

No one really gets the full picture of a candidate in an interview	An interview only needs to reveal just enough information to get you the job.
Panel interviews give you totally unpredictable results	Sitting in front of an interview panel can be a headache – see Chapter 14 – but there are predictable questions and interviewer behaviours.
It's all about personality	Every interview is about trying to visualise you working in a particular context, and it does matter how well you fit into a team. However, what you do and know matters too.
Getting 'no' all the time means you are probably not going to get a job	Sounds like a good excuse for giving up. Don't accept random results as meaningful feedback – see Chapters 19 and 20.
Interviewers know what they are doing	Sometimes true, sometimes entirely untrue, which is why it is so dangerous to accept rejection letters as a true indication of your ability.
Repeated failure usually means that you are in for a long search	Or it could mean that you need to rethink your strategy. Banging your head against the same wall, the same way, is not a great long-term approach.
It's all about who you know – the interview is just for show	Employers always prefer candidates they know something about, but they are curious about talent that might be out there, untapped. It's your job to establish a relationship quickly so you become a known quantity.

CHAPTER TWO

Why do interviews go wrong?

THIS CHAPTER LOOKS AT:

- What typically goes wrong, and why
- The misguided assumptions we make about interview results
- Seeing the difference between long shots and near-misses
- The 10 per cent rule
- What decision makers say about the process

NOT QUITE THE RESULT I WAS LOOKING FOR …

Having looked at what a great performance looks like, time for some diagnostics about what can go wrong. Interviews do sometimes get you unpredictable results. If you knew exactly why, you'd adjust your performance unassisted and you wouldn't need this book.

Some activities in life are fairly predictable, but job interviews present several multiple, mysterious realities:

- Questions came up that you didn't expect.
- You found it difficult to think up good examples under pressure.

- The interviewer did all the talking.

- You didn't get a chance to talk about the things you had in mind.

- The interviewer seemed to be talking about a different job to the one you applied for.

- You never really warmed up.

- It seemed to go brilliantly but you never heard anything again.

- It went OK, but you aren't sure that the interviewer will remember you.

Even experienced workers or people who have been on the job market for a long time are not terribly good at interpreting what happened in an interview. Candidates often say 'it was a terrible interview' and get invited back, while others say 'it went like a dream' and get an impersonal rejection letter.

JOINING THE DOTS

Just as frustrated authors collect rejection slips from publishers, some candidates proudly count 'no' letters. When an employer is sifting paper applications, the chances of getting short listed are always pretty small if the field of applicants is large. If there are 500-plus people chasing a job the odds are against getting an interview, no matter how brilliant your application is. That's an important reality check that cuts through the randomness of the job market (but see Chapter 19 for more on your job search 'statistics').

'There are two types of interview', explains career consultant Robin Rose. 'The first is a structured interview, probably by a HR professional, which looks in detail at skills required for the job. This is essentially for ruling people out. If you can match the basic requirements of the job you can probably get through this without difficulty; the second is a *selection* interview where the criteria are not about skills and experience but about why you should be offered the job. In the second type, a positive attitude really matters.'

Second-guessing a recruitment decision is a slippery game. With a lack of real evidence, you may draw your own, wrong, conclusions. If you get a 'no' letter it's very tempting to believe you can join the dots and decide how and why you didn't get an offer. You might blame the lack of professionalism of the interviewer. Even more likely, you will blame yourself: 'I don't interview well' is a far more common statement than you might think.

SEEING THE DIFFERENCE BETWEEN 'NO' AND 'NEARLY YES'

There is a big difference between an interview that rules you out, and one that very nearly rules you in. Don't read more into the interview result than you actually see. You may have put in a convincing performance but just lacked a little bit of sector knowledge. You may have been up against an internal candidate who was informally promised the job 18 months ago. Let's be clear: *most times the real reasons for hiring decisions will always be completely hidden from you.*

The offer of an interview probably means that you have the skills and knowledge to do the job, but sometimes with more junior jobs these things are not tested until you are in the room. So if your interview feedback is 'post holders need the European Computer Driving Licence', it's a good reminder to:

1 double check employer requirements in advance;

2 either get the minimum qualifications you need or learn to talk about appropriate, equivalent experience.

THE 10 PER CENT RULE

New businesses are often founded on an interesting principle. You don't have to invent a completely new service or product, and you can even set up in direct competition with other businesses, as long as you offer something that is different by 10 per cent – you might be 10 per cent faster, cheaper, better quality. That 10 per cent is enough edge.

The same rule applies to improved job interview performance. Think of a recent interview experience. If you were able to answer all questions positively and clearly with good evidence, then the job probably fits the 'nearly yes' category. Well done. That means you are getting results. You probably don't need to reshape what you do, but next time you need to do something 10 per cent better – better answers, better voice, better body language, better evidence. Small changes have huge leverage.

WHY DO PEOPLE (STILL) GET INTERVIEWS WRONG?

The nation's favourite interview strategy is still 'I'll wing it'. This often means 'I don't know what they will ask me but I will just be myself'.

Imagine your boss invites you to a meeting next month about your long-term prospects. This meeting will have a big impact on the next stage of your career. No sensible person would go into that meeting without being prepared to talk about achievements, special skills and knowledge, preferred working conditions, and the future. Job interviews often have the same life impact, yet we approach them planning to improvise.

WHAT GOES WRONG?

Candidates are notoriously poor at judging their own performance in all kinds of assessments, including interviews. So, whether you thought it was a good or bad interview may not be relevant. You have no idea who you are up against, and probably only half an idea of what the interviewer is looking for. Don't get stuck in 'if only' mode: 'If only I had more experience, better qualifications, more confidence ...' Behind this wish to reinvent yourself is a huge misunderstanding – that an employer is looking for, and will find, the perfect candidate. All recruitment is a compromise – employers rarely get exactly what they are looking for. Recruiters will tell you that the person who gets hired is the one who matches most areas. In addition, it is not always the best candidate who gets the job, it is often the person who performs best at interview.

Who is well placed to answer the question about what typically goes wrong in a job interview? Employers. Sometimes it's an HR perspective, but the most important viewpoint is that of a line manager or business owner – in other words, someone whose success depends on a good appointment.

Successive surveys point to a staggeringly obvious fact. Employers keep meeting candidates who have not organised themselves for the interview. This comes through in a number of ways:

1   Failure to organise the *application* – candidates are not sure what CV they used, what forms they have completed, or which job they are applying for.

2   Failure to organise *research* – on the requirements of the job and the nature of the organisation. Candidates just haven't thought about the employer's wish list.

3   Failure to organise *self* – presentation, dress, manner, attitude, speaking style. Candidates just haven't thought enough about the way they will come across.

4   Failure to organise *evidence* – of skills, achievements, failures, high points. Candidates just haven't thought enough about what they have done.

These four critical areas are all dealt with in depth in the chapters ahead. However, when pressed further, employers often zoom in on one critical factor – evidence.

DIFFERING PERSPECTIVES ON EVIDENCE

Having spent about a quarter of a century training interviewers and nearly as much time debriefing candidates after job interviews, it's hard not to keep a mental checklist of the things that come up all the time.

The odd thing is that these change very rarely, even if jobs are scarce or good candidates are hard to find. Employers and candidates tend to say the same things repeatedly, and it's interesting that they are often two sides of the same coin:

WHAT CANDIDATES SAY 'Interviewers don't …'	WHAT EMPLOYERS SAY 'Candidates don't …'
● Explain what the role and organisation is about.	● Match their experience to the requirements of the role.
● Show much interest in me as a candidate.	● Find out the basics of what we do here.
● Ask about my strengths and achievements.	● Have anything to say about their career highlights.
● Spend time getting to know me as a person.	● Have a clear explanation for their work history and career development.
● Understand my background.	● Make their skills sound transferable by using language that we recognise.

WHAT CANDIDATES SAY 'Interviewers don't ...'	WHAT EMPLOYERS SAY 'Candidates don't ...'
● Ask relevant questions about my work history.	● Prepare evidence that goes beyond what is on their CV.
● Give me a chance to show my enthusiasm for the job.	● Show enthusiasm for the job or the organisation.
● Explain exactly what they are looking for.	● Have a clear reason why they want the job.
● Tell me the topics that will come up in questions.	● Understand why we are hiring.
● Help me understand how I can fit the role.	● Understand what we might be looking for in the ideal candidate.
● Give timely or useful feedback on the interview process.	● Have smart questions for us.

The picture is often mirrored, but there is an important difference between the two. It is an employer's job to make the interview go well; it is your job to make the interview *go well for you*. To complain that an interviewer didn't give you the chance to talk, didn't want to hear about your achievements or didn't discover your secret talents is rather like an aggrieved politician complaining that in a TV interview he was asked all the wrong questions. It's your job to get the key evidence across, *whether the question is asked or not*.

That may sound unrealistic or feel pushy, but it isn't – it's just about recognising that you need to decide from the outset to put in an above-average performance, and to do that you need an above-average mindset. You need to decide in advance that you are not going to make the mistakes that others make, that you are not going to be the kind of 'problem' candidate who makes an interviewer's life difficult. You are going to be the kind of candidate an employer wants to retain, even if there isn't a job available right now.

THE BASIC EMPLOYER SHORT LIST

Before we get too deep into the candidate mindset, do remember that employers are not terribly sophisticated in their decision making. The US National Association of Colleges and Employers in 2010 published a list of five top skills required by employers (the Association of Graduate Recruiters in the UK has a similar checklist). Where have you demonstrated these skills and qualities?

1   Verbal and written communication skills

2   Strong work ethic

3   Teamwork skills

4   Analytical skills

5   Initiative.

Employers surveyed also valued interpersonal skills, flexibility and adaptability, computer and organisational skills. The interesting thing is that employers still feel the need, even in a recession, to spell out these basic requirements. It cannot be the case that candidates do not possess most of these qualities. It is far more likely that they *do not know how to communicate them*.

I GET THE INTERVIEWS BUT NOT THE JOB

It's a common problem. There are individuals out there who do brilliantly on paper, nearly always get short listed, but don't seem to get the right results. Many candidates never get beyond an uncomfortably formal exchange of information. They make every answer sound pre-rehearsed, and not always exactly related to the question. At the end, the interviewer feels like an information download has occurred, but it hasn't felt in any sense like a conversation.

Make a clear distinction between wild shots and likely hits. Random applications for jobs you have little to offer will always give you random and confusing results. However, if you are genuinely getting interviews for the sort of job you could do well, where you really do have relevant skills, qualifications and motivation, and you are constantly getting rejection letters (Chapter 19 tackles this topic in depth), you need to think about doing something differently. Notice that phrase: *think about doing something differently*. As outlined above, this doesn't mean a complete overhaul – small tweaks to your performance may be enough. Starting to think differently means not just doing all the right things, but doing them much more consciously, seeking an edge at every point. Read on to see how.

CHAPTER THREE

How do I handle interviews with recruitment consultants?

THIS CHAPTER LOOKS AT:

- What recruitment agencies can, realistically, do for you
- Interpreting the feedback they give you
- Building relationships to increase your chances of being short listed
- The insider view – tips from an executive recruiter

THE WORLD OF THE RECRUITMENT AGENCY

A significant number of jobs are filled by agencies, connecting job seekers with employers. They rarely call themselves 'employment agencies', which they are in law, but use other terms including 'recruitment consultancy', 'staff suppliers', 'search' or 'search and selection consultancy', or 'headhunters'. These businesses operate in different styles and at different ends of the market, but they all have one thing in common: they make a charge to employers for putting people into jobs. Some agencies also place large numbers of temporary workers, and others handle interim managers.

They are an important part of your job search. They are an even more important part of your interviewing experience. Agencies screen candidates so that employers don't have to, and very often this involves a telephone interview (see Chapter 14) or a face-to-face interview.

Recruitment expert Shirley Howe offers this advice, based on her wide experience: 'Agency recruiters are focused on the hard core skills. Because most of them will have never done the job themselves, they will work on logical lists to check the candidate ticks all the boxes and has the required amount of experience. The hiring manager on the other hand has generally done the job themselves, or has a very good understanding of what is required. They will be going on their "gut" reaction as to whether they like the person and if they will fit in their team. They won't necessarily be so concerned with skills, as they will be able to tell from some very simple questions if the person has them.'

Interviews with recruitment consultants vary in terms of structure and quality as much as employer interviews. Some candidates make the mistake of thinking it's 'only' an agency interview, but there are important reasons to take agency interviews seriously, and a number of factors which should shape your thinking.

WHAT AGENCIES CAN DO FOR YOU

● No matter how well an agency looks after candidates, ultimately its responsibility is to fit people into jobs and fulfil an employer's needs. You may receive helpful career advice in passing, but it's not guaranteed.

● Get your message across quickly and succinctly when talking to recruitment consultants – if you can say what you offer and are looking for in under two minutes you'll get their attention.

- The recruiter is being the eyes and ears of the employer in these circumstances and a strong recommendation may push you right through to a job offer.

- Professional recruitment consultants have often spent a great deal of time analysing job requirements, so can give you detailed information about how far your profile matches the job.

- If an agency decides to put you forward, you should ask for tips and guidance about ways to strengthen your position. Ask the recruiter to help you understand what the employer is really looking for beneath the surface of the job description.

- Your recruitment consultant will have spent a great deal of time building a relationship with the decision-maker, so should be able to advise you about the kind of people who will be interviewing you at the next stage.

- If you make a good impression as an employable candidate, the agency may have other options to offer you. In some circumstances they will also recommend other agencies, or good career coaches.

- With exceptionally strong candidates agencies are often able to press hard on points such as job content, salary and timing. If you are very marketable, an agency may persuade an employer to create a job around you.

- An agency will always have more leverage than you in persuading an employer to commit to decisions about short listing, interview dates and job offers.

- Agencies can often offer employers flexible means of solving problems, including temporary or short-term appointments. Don't be surprised if you are asked about these ways of working.

- Recruitment specialists of this kind really understand

the market, or at least the sectors they work in. They can therefore give you good advice about what employers are looking for.

WHAT AGENCIES CANNOT DO FOR YOU

- Agencies are relatively intolerant of poor fit. If you are lacking in key experience, they'll tell you pretty fast. You will need a strong 'pitch' to get past these issues.

- They are relatively conservative – the perfect candidate for them is one who has done the job before. However, if you build relationships they can sometimes help you change sector.

- Remember that agencies are overwhelmed by hopeful candidates, particularly in a tough market. There is no point approaching an agency that is *never* going to handle the kind of role you're after.

- If you fail to make a good impression or to take the interview seriously, it's unlikely the agency will deal with you further unless you are exceptionally employable.

- They can coach you before an employer interview, but can't guarantee you the job.

FOLLOW-UP FROM AGENCIES

- After an agency has talked to you, you may get a quick response, or it may take some time for the employer to decide on a final short list. Don't read anything into delays – things can sometimes take a long time.

- Occasionally you may hear nothing at all – the willingness of agencies to deal professionally with candidates is notoriously varied.

- Since these recruiters interview candidates all the time, they are often in a position to give good feedback.

RECRUITMENT CONSULTANT FEEDBACK

The last point needs special attention. The feedback you get from recruitment consultants might be the best you ever receive, or might be very slanted to the agency's perspective. Sometimes they have a distorted picture of how many jobs are available because in a recession employers can often fill jobs without their assistance. Consultants often have strong views about CV format. They usually dislike CV profiles (they want your job history unfiltered so they can 'sell' you to an employer, but it's still true that a good profile helps in a CV you send directly to employers). Sometimes they have hard and fast interview rules ('always/never wear a white shirt/brown shoes/earrings/a trouser suit ...'). These 'rules', like all advice, should be cross-checked against what others recommend, and *what works for you and the company that is recruiting you.*

External recruiters are busy people and want to understand what you have to offer quickly. Because they want employers to commit, they are highly tuned to employer buy-in, and can persuade employers to make a final job offer decision.

However, where recruitment consultants often excel is in giving candidates no-frills advice about how they come across at interview – advice to take seriously. An executive recruiter told me about sending a candidate to be interviewed by a CEO, who fed back that the panel were 'exhausted' after the interview and felt completely drained because this candidate talked incessantly. Afterwards the candidate admitted that he completely forgot his coaching on brevity. A tough feedback session followed – this candidate's habitual over-delivery and its impact on others were seriously getting in the way of his career prospects.

Judith Armatage, Director of Professional Development at the Recruitment & Employment Confederation adds: 'A good interview with a trained recruiter can be invaluable – allowing the work seeker to uncover previously unacknowledged skills and the depth of those skills. It should establish the motivations for any job move and importantly establish the key criteria for the next role. An agency interview can also open up new opportunities in terms of flexible working through temporary or contract opportunities.'

RELATIONSHIPS MATTER

Recruitment consultants are essentially relationship driven. If you think about it, it's obvious. The main part of their job is a consultative sales role, persuading an employer to give them a vacancy to fill. This requires a high level of people and influencing skills. So these are the qualities they respect most in others.

So, like most things in life, who you know can get you through the door and recruitment agencies are no exception. They are far more likely to take your call if you are being recommended by someone who gives them business. So if you know someone who works in HR ask them to recommend someone in the recruitment world.

You need to work hard to get an agency on your side. One consultant summarised short listing: 'We typically offer four to five candidates to an employer. Candidates one to four will be pretty much identikit matches, but candidate five may have a slightly unusual background with experience in a different sector. This candidate is slightly different from the profile, but one who will impress.'

Another recruiter admitted recently: 'When I drive home every evening having interviewed between five and eight candidates a day, I ask myself *who can I remember?* On a good day it's usually no more than two.' Busy recruiters often ask candidates to register on a database, but in reality they only turn to it if they are bored or desperate – most short lists are filled with people the recruiter has spoken to recently. Don't pester, but do maintain relationships with recruiters – by voice, rather than by email. Often an updated CV is a good reason to call.

So, if you are trying to work with an agency and you are advised to 'email in your CV', do realise that you have not moved up to first base yet, at least in relationship terms. If you are told to 'register on the website' that really means 'we haven't begun any kind of conversation with you yet'. Ask for opportunities to speak to actual consultants handling the kind of job you are seeking, and ask them detailed questions about the job. Above all else, however, try to strike up some kind of personal rapport by taking whatever opportunity you can for a face-to-face conversation.

Finally, even if your recruitment consultant is half your age and seems to be giving you very basic advice, don't be arrogant or complacent, or treat the occasion as uninspiringly routine. Don't let your doubts about recruitment consultancies or agencies influence this one interview or decision. Agencies need a flow of enthusiastic, committed candidates.

BEING INTERVIEWED BY A RECRUITMENT CONSULTANT

So, what matters in this kind of interview? A small amount of content, and a large amount of trust. You wouldn't be getting an interview if you didn't have at least some of the skills and experience required, so what matters now is answering two big questions in the recruitment consultant's mind: (1) 'Can I place this person?' and (2) 'Will this person get an uncomplicated YES at interview?' Therefore it really matters that you take a recruiter interview just as seriously as the real thing, and give detailed, memorable answers to (1) and send off a whole range of positive signals confirming (2).

View from an executive recruiter

DO

- Take time to establish rapport with the interviewer.

- Prepare well for the obvious questions: why you want this job, what you'll bring, evidence for competencies/experience outlined in the advert/job spec.

- Listen to the question – don't just launch into a summary of your career if that's not what you're asked for.

- Make the best of the time you have available – if you're asked to give a 5-minute overview of your career don't take 40 minutes as this will take time away from other areas the interviewer may need to probe.

- Ensure your enthusiasm for the role comes across – the interviewer will be keen to determine your motivation.

- Read their body language. For example, if you have just said something which has surprised or concerned them you may see the interviewer become suddenly more attentive – if you see this, clarify what you are saying. On the other hand, if the interviewer's attention shifts to the paperwork you probably need to wrap up.

Think of a few questions you could ask the interviewer to demonstrate your interest.

DON'T

- Be afraid of silence – take the time you need to think of the best example or answer for a particular question.

- Rush the small talk – this is a crucial way of establishing rapport and gives the interviewer an opportunity to see what you're like socially and personally.

- Refer to the same particular experience in response to too many questions – draw on other examples.

Joëlle Warren, Executive Chairman, Warren Partners

CHAPTER FOUR

How do I move from short list to interview?

THIS CHAPTER LOOKS AT:

- How short listing isn't half as accurate as you thought it was
- Improved strategies for getting past the short list stage
- Spotting the deal-breakers
- Getting the language right

THE ROUGH ART OF SHORT LISTING

It's expensive to take senior staff away from other duties and put them in an interview room, so organisations need to reduce a long list of applicants down to a small number who will be called for interview – the short list.

Textbooks on recruitment and selection underline the importance of objective and fair pre-selection, or short listing. As soon as real people are involved this becomes a rather uncertain business. The aim is 100 per cent perfect prediction, but actual results are a long way off that, even using tests and structured interviews.

Some methods (such as references) give results much closer to pure chance. If you're in an interview being asked bizarre questions, fired at you by someone who isn't really listening to your answers, you might like to know that the predictive power of an unstructured interview is not significantly greater than random selection.

Occupational psychologists admit that there is no sure-fire way of predicting how someone will perform on the job in the long term just by examining the evidence candidates present on paper and in person. Some factors, particularly long-term motivation, are very hard to measure.

Thankfully, selectors are usually objective enough to focus with some clarity on the skills and attributes that will be a pretty good match to the job. However, the selection process is not a perfect way of assessing people, which is why you need to think carefully about how you listen to feedback (see Chapter 20).

Employers don't need perfect candidates; a recruiter's real goal is *the best person in the best time at the best cost*. Your job is to stand out enough from the short list to move to the interview stage, avoiding the classic mistakes made by those many job seekers who do everything they possibly can *not* to stand out from the crowd.

'SIX FOR SIX'

Many recruiters say they spend less than 20 seconds assessing a CV. That means you have to make an impact FAST. The key here is to make it easy for the recruiter to spot your key messages so that your CV ends up in the right pile on the recruiter's desk.

Your standard CV will probably start with a short profile highlighting what you want people to remember about you. Then hopefully you will have a list of skills, achievements and other factors which are likely to hit the high value items on the employer's shopping list. So far so good.

But here's where one of those small changes can make all the difference between an invitation to interview and a swift journey to the bin. The insider secret is that what your potential employer is really looking for as they sift through the big pile on their desk, are the 'deal-breaker' elements. These boil down to between 6 and 10 requirements – beyond that is the realm of 'nice to have'.

If you just send your standard CV, you are leaving it to chance that your list of skills happens to include the recruiter's wish list. That isn't smart practice. It is crucial to tailor your CV and covering letter so that you stand out as the candidate who is delivering all of their six big ticket items.

Sounds too simple? You would be amazed how many applications fail to play the 'six for six' game. It's also an excellent way of working on your primary messages at interview (see Chapter 12).

THE TOP 10 REASONS CVS ARE REJECTED

If an interview goes wrong, it could be for a thousand different reasons but the chances are it will be one of the factors identified in Chapter 2 and elsewhere in this book. The same is true for CVs – if you're not getting short listed, the probability is that your CV is letting you down for one or more of the following reasons which regularly come up in surveys of what employers find off-putting:

1 Your CV is not tailored to the role – either in terms of content (right skills and knowledge) or style (the information is hard to find and not in language an employer finds easy to buy into). Avoid impenetrable acronyms or jargon.

2 The first 30 words of your CV send out the wrong summary message – for example, starting with a job title which limits your options. Younger applicants tend to write far too much about their qualifications and not enough about skills.

3 Many CVs over-sell, sometimes embarrassingly. Avoid empty adjectives, CV clichés ('individualist but also a team player'); focus on what you have done rather than what you think you are like.

4 Over-delivery is a major problem. Two pages is ideal, three is acceptable, but make sure that your key messages are in the first two-thirds of page one. The best CVs get your five or six most suitable pieces of evidence across quickly; the worst are full of irrelevant data.

5 Over-fussy presentation – coloured paper, mixed fonts, fancy text effects. Use a simple layout with plenty of white space. Use bullet points, vary them in length, and start sentences with energetic verbs (e.g. 'Led ...' or 'Initiated ...').

6 Weaker CVs tend to be a rehash of past job descriptions. Stronger ones write about achievements and show what you added to each role.

7 However, employers quickly feel jaded if you over-egg skills and achievements – back up your claims with hard evidence.

8 Don't waste space and ink listing skills which could be performed by someone much more junior than you.

9 Look again at your CV profile. Employers dislike profiles if they are full of self-praise, but appreciate ones which say who you are, what you have done, and where you'd like your career to go next.

10 Missing details (show what you got out of gap years, for example), presenting a career history as disjointed (if you had a series of short-term positions write about them as a joined-up career phase, emphasising learning and sector experience); stressing the wrong information (e.g. too much emphasis on your family commitments).

READING THE CLUES – SPOTTING DEAL-BREAKERS

Use all the information at your disposal to interpret what an employer is really looking for. Start with job documents, but learn to read between the lines (get someone experienced to help). The simple rule here is that *employers always ask for more than they can assess*. It's vital you realise that, so you can focus your preparation time on those things which will make the biggest difference to success or failure.

How can you interrogate job information effectively? Look at the list of competencies, skills, experience and other factors required for the role.

Your next step is to work out weighting – in other words, what are the 'must have' factors that an employer believes are deal-breakers? If you are unsure, examine which points are given maximum attention in the job advertisement; since it's a lot shorter than the job description, key elements are easier to spot.

Ask yourself how the job could have been described differently. When a job is advertised in print or on the Internet, conscious decisions have been made about what information is left in or out. Some terms are included to make the advertisement attractive, other items are clear indications of deal-breakers. What is given particular emphasis? What is missing? You need to decide whether you have enough material to match, and assuming you do, make sure you pitch your message accordingly, both in your cover letter and at interview.

Next there are the discretionary things that an employer would be pleased to have but can live without. Match them if you can, but not at the expense of good evidence linked to the 'must have' list. You might also think of things you can offer which are not on the employer's wish list. Don't go overboard here, but there may be strong ingredients in your mix that are not only relevant, but could mark you out as having something extra.

Supplement your review of job documents with any 'live' information you can pick up through contacts or by talking to the organisation. Who do you know who has worked at the same place or is a supplier, consultant, in the same sector? Remember you are *not* attempting to push yourself forward at this stage, just to find out enough about the job to have a more secure target to aim at. One of the best pieces of information you can fall across is to find out what kind of person held the job beforehand. For example, if the last person took a lot of risks and things didn't work out, the chances are that this time the employer is seeking a safe pair of hands. If the last post holder was an internal candidate who didn't shine, the chances are much higher that an external candidate will get the job.

Some job ads explicitly offer a contact person for questions. Use this conversation for exactly that – there is no point trying to sell yourself into an interview at this stage, but you will be remembered if you ask intelligent questions. Employers are irritated by candidates who try to push themselves onto a short list by asking for special consideration. Always remember, in their eyes it's not about what you want, it's about what they need. They aren't going to care if you've been looking for a job for ages, or you have a holiday booked, or you have another pressing job offer (although the last one may make you seem more desirable).

If the job is being handled by a recruitment agency, ask a complicated or technical question about the job. This means you will probably get a chance to speak to the consultant handling the job rather than the first person to pick up the phone. When you speak to the consultant work hard at establishing a warm working relationship – try to drop one or two pieces of information into the conversation that will help you be remembered.

LANGUAGE

A point that relates as much to interviews as short listing is to find the right language. You will have heard a lot about transferable skills, and probably wonder if you have any. In fact your skills only become transferable if you describe them in a way that a busy employer finds attractive. Research conducted by the website Gumtree in August 2010 indicated that 52 per cent of employers found that applicants did not identify relevant skills when they were trying to change sectors.

It may surprise you to know that most people are not good at identifying their skills. They tend to undervalue what they do well, only describe the skills valued by their current employer, and ignore the skills used outside work. Learn to *translate* your skills – skills only become 'transferable' when an employer spots them, understands them, and then buys into them. Your job is to make that happen. Employers often complain that candidates use jargon or describe their skills in terms used in another sector. Look carefully at the language the employer uses on its website and elsewhere in describing roles and functions. Ask the advice of people with sector knowledge: 'How do I describe my experience in a way that makes me sound like an inside track candidate?'

You get three main chances to communicate your skills: (1) in your CV, (2) in conversations with people who can help you, and (3) in a job interview. Remember, it's not what you have done, but how you sell your experience – so use active language like 'led', 'organised', 'built'. Avoid making hollow-sounding claims about your skills ('I am a self-starter') but give clear evidence – times you used your skills, and what happened as a result.

Research on social interaction points us to the importance of *mirroring*. Much of this is expressed in body language where we find ourselves adopting the same postures as someone we get on with. Mirroring also occurs in the words we speak – a conversation is often successful if we match the speaking style of the other person. At interview you're given big clues about the language to use to describe your skills and experience. So, if someone is using technical language, use it in return. If someone is speaking formally, you need to be less casual.

FROM SHORT LIST TO THE BIG DAY

In an interview, you find yourself trusting in a number of things – your CV, your work history, your skills. Sadly some candidates forget an important truth: the reason that people don't do well at interview is far more often about what happens in the interview room than your past experience.

So, first of all, give yourself a pat on the back for getting this far. Getting an interview means you already have evidence that you match at least three-quarters of the employer's requirements. Having won through the short list by matching your experience to the job, you will have to repeat the process at interview. Careers specialist Malcolm Watt states that 'Most people go into an interview nervous of the outcome and thinking they have a mountain to climb before they achieve a job offer', adding that 'getting an interview puts you more than half way up the mountain – you wouldn't be in the interview if they didn't think you could do the job.'

So now you can build on the well-presented evidence that has got you past stage one, and move into interview mode. When you get there, what you have to do is to relax just enough to reveal the rest, including the right degree of confidence and the ability to get on with people.

Now you also need to get your head in the right place …

CHAPTER FIVE

Handling interview nerves

THIS CHAPTER LOOKS AT:

- Ways that nervousness can hide your potential
- Reasons why being nervous can be helpful
- How routine advice probably won't help
- Tips to overcome the worst of interview nerves

WHAT IF I AM (VERY) NERVOUS?

Most interview books tell you that being nervous is a good thing because it raises your attentiveness and shows that you care about the process. True enough, but no one should underestimate how nerves can block what you want to achieve at interview. Interestingly, interviewers are often nervous, too, particularly if they are working alongside someone senior or more experienced. Young people who have little experience of being interviewed are often anxious about the process (and some of them need to be more so), but interview nerves go through the age spectrum. Why? Because often an interview really matters – it can mean the difference between certainty and uncertainty, the ability to make plans, a next step that could reshape your career. Even more critically, it's about *you*. Presenting a product or organisation is one thing, talking about yourself is completely different – which is why even the most senior people get nervous.

The real downside, as Rebecca Alexander of *Psychologies* magazine recently pointed out to me, is that fear makes us avoid thinking about the details of the process. Candidates do better if they picture themselves in each stage of a selection process, visualising how they will behave. This is not done as frequently as it should be, but is a great way of anticipating the demands of the process ahead and planning how you will be, as well as what you will say. However, for many people, visualising what will happen can make them feel even more anxious, so they hide from what is coming and miss a powerful way to prepare for a great interview.

For some people just being asked to speak in an interview is an ordeal. Take comfort from the fact that a large number of accomplished performers – public speakers, business leaders, actors – are secretly terrified. Sir Laurence Olivier, even at the height of his career, used to be physically sick before he walked on stage.

SYMPTOMS THAT GET IN THE WAY

Even the most experienced professionals can experience the following symptoms:

- A mouth that becomes so dry you can hardly speak.

- Worrying that you will not remember the things you need to say.

- A sudden inability to make small talk.

- Unsteady, shaking hands, sticky palms, raised heartbeat, nausea.

- A racing mind which prevents you hearing the questions asked.

- Saying too much about the wrong things, or too little about what matters.

- Clumsiness – the ability to knock over anything in range.

- A feeling that everything you say 'comes out wrong'.

- Difficulties reading your notes or recollecting examples under pressure.

- Difficulty talking positively about yourself.

- A growing sense that you are a fake.

These are real symptoms and not to be dismissed or overcome easily. They arise from a very old part of the human brain which governs primordial responses like blushing, heartbeat and breathing – those times when your body takes over no matter how hard you concentrate. Remember that fear fires up adrenaline, which also improves your performance, so in a way you can welcome the symptoms, because they are a clear sign that your brain is kicking into gear.

MANAGING INTERVIEW NERVES

There isn't a magic bullet, but there are things you can do. Start by taking a gradual approach, dealing with one worry at a time and learning from a few tried and tested strategies. Look at the list below, and also write down any additional symptoms you experience under interview pressure. Now score each item from 1 (not too worrying) to 5 (this really gets in the way), then think about what you can do to improve the situation. Tip: start on the number 1 scores first – start to teach your unconscious brain a few lessons about managing under pressure.

SYMPTOM	YOUR SCORE 1–5	SUGGESTED STRATEGY
Dry mouth		Water won't touch it. Eat a boiled sweet or drink a sugary black coffee before you begin – sugar coats the mouth and works much better than water, which you will probably spill.
I never remember the things I want to say		Preparing things in short chunks helps.
Unsteady, shaking hands		If you are offered a drink, say no. The sound of a cup rattling in a saucer is unmistakeable. You will probably end up wearing your drink.
Sticky palms		You can buy anti-perspirant for hands in spray and cream form, which also prevents a damp handshake.
Raised heartbeat, nausea		Learn some relaxation techniques, but if you do nothing else, do some deep, slow breathing before you begin.
A racing mind		This is a positive, because it's a sign that adrenaline is helping you fire on all cylinders. Preparing your material and answers in advance should reassure you that this is something you can live with.

SYMPTOM	YOUR SCORE 1–5	SUGGESTED STRATEGY
Not hearing the questions asked		You have heard them, it's just that your brain wants to gallop into the next pre-prepared speech. Learn to listen to the exact words of the question, and then for the short silence at the end of it. It's perfectly acceptable to pause before beginning a detailed answer.
Foot-in-mouth disease – every time I try to give a good example I drop myself in it		Take comfort – you are going to do enough work before the interview so that you will know what you will say before you open your mouth.
Clamming up		Not saying enough will often keep you off the final short list. Decide in advance what three or four critical points you want to get across.
Clumsiness		Move slowly, and don't carry things that you will drop or fall over.
Mumbling		Interviewers often complain that candidates give half their answers in an undertone, a mumbled throw-away line, which is sometimes supposed to be ironic. Say only the things that you think will score you points, and don't add half-formed statements.

▶

SYMPTOM	YOUR SCORE 1–5	SUGGESTED STRATEGY
A feeling that everything you say sounds odd and inadequate		Rehearse your opening statements, small talk, and your mini-narratives carefully. Practice not only gives you instant access to material, but also makes sure messages come out the way you intend.
I need notes to remind me of my answers and I can't read them quickly		You won't need notes after a little practice because you will have learned a number of micro-sequences that will come out naturally if prompted, but if you do need notes to help draw symbols or cartoons in the margin of your CV – they are easier to follow under pressure.
Difficulties recollecting examples under pressure		The only way to deal with this is to do the work (recollection, filtering and editing) way, way in advance of the interview.
I go to pieces doing presentations		Chapter 9 is designed to make sure you don't. A presentation is a gift – a fantastic opportunity to show how you will perform in the role. Questions raised during your presentation show that your audience is listening and buying in to what you have to offer.

SYMPTOM	YOUR SCORE 1–5	SUGGESTED STRATEGY
A sudden inability to make small talk		Decide in advance what you might talk about. React naturally, smile, don't over-deliver or start making speeches.
A growing sense that you are a fake		A number of people feel they are 'faking it' at work, let alone during the interview. You wouldn't be in the interview if you didn't have the potential to do the job.

'JUST BE YOURSELF'

This is the advice you will probably hear before every interview. How irritating that phrase is, failing to acknowledge how vulnerable you feel when someone turns the spotlight on you. Not only that, it's frustratingly difficult to achieve. As if there was a switch in your head marked 'myself – On/Off'. It's well-meant advice, but almost meaningless. We are different selves in different areas of our lives – when we are with partners, family, close friends, in public, with colleagues, with the boss. Which 'myself' are you supposed to be?

The self you reveal at interview will always be a slightly more anxious, restrained, cautious version of you, and it's misleading to pretend otherwise. And interviewers realise this. They know that the person they meet in the interview is not an exact replica of the way you will be at work. It's their job to get you to disclose enough of yourself to make a selection decision. So, while you can't just 'be yourself', it is your job to give them enough to show them a positive version of yourself as the right choice for the job.

How?

1 Get help from a coach or from friends to capture that person – *you on a good day*. What puts you in the right frame of mind to be that kind of person? For some people, rediscovering this energised, alternative 'you' just before an interview can make a huge difference.

2 Do whatever you need to do (see Chapter 6) to be a switched on, positive, attentive but slightly anxious version of you. That will work just fine.

3 As daunting as it is to anticipate questions, having a ready bank of evidence builds confidence considerably.

4 Warm up mentally by thinking and talking about positive things in the 30 minutes before an interview; you'll find it makes an enormous difference to your state of mind, especially if you are a modest, slow starter.

Remember, all you are trying to do is allow an interviewer enough glimpses to imagine you in the job. You don't have to totally defeat your nerves to achieve this, just distract them for a while, and kid them into allowing you to reveal an employable self.

'JUST RELAX'

This is the second most irritating piece of advice. You hear the same from the dentist just as he reaches for something sharp. You are, of course, the opposite of relaxed, so it's rather like saying 'don't look down' at the top of a skyscraper.

The phrase is also used, misleadingly, when interviewers say 'relax – it's just a chat'. Whether it's lunch, coffee or an 'informal' discussion, it's always an interview, and you should always prepare as if it is.

However, when someone says 'relax', what you should

hear is 'make my job easier'. An interviewer needs to get you to disclose information, some of it relatively personal. If you disclose the right things in the right way, it's difficult not to get a result. So smile and breathe deeply, because you're trying to help someone do their job.

For some people who display more than half a dozen of the nervousness symptoms outlined above, it pays to learn some kind of relaxation system such as relaxation tapes, relieving muscle tension, or meditation. There are as many ways of doing this as there are nervous interviewees, but the interesting thing is that you probably already know what works for you, and you avoid doing it because that means getting to grips with the problem.

START FROM STILLNESS

Do you look agitated or calm at the beginning of an interview? Look at politicians. The ones who are trusted the most are often the ones with *gravitas* – that old-fashioned word which describes a calm, dignified presence. They begin an interview sitting straight, looking attentive rather than formally stiff. They look around slowly at what is going on in the room, weighing things up. Even though they may be nervous, they don't look it because their body movements are slow and controlled. When asked a question, they respond in a measured, clear way rather than rushing into the answer. As they speak, they command attention and 'hold the floor' for a few moments. Their answer ends audibly, too – you can almost hear the full stop.

Work towards an interview presence which begins in stillness – particularly important if you are slightly agitated, fidgeting or pulling at your collar or hemline, perhaps talking too fast. Practise sitting. Sit in a position which is comfortable but where your balance is tipped slightly forward, with one foot slightly forward of the other, exactly as you would if you were holding yourself ready to stand quickly in one smooth movement. Keep your hands still by holding a document folder. Look forward, and release any tension in your neck and shoulders. Breathe in slowly and gently, for longer than you would do normally, and release your breath slowly. This technique will improve the strength and depth of your voice (both factors which impress) as well as relaxing you.

Listen, too. Listen to the volume that other people speak at, because this is the best clue you'll get about your own delivery volume.

Sitting and breathing and listening – is that it? It also helps if you can do something to still the racing mind at the same time. Breathing is often enough, but if you have some other meditative technique that helps you be still mentally as well as physically, use it now. It might be a repeated phrase like 'calm, calm, calm'. It might be visualising a place and time when you were quietly happy. Be still, and wait for the first question.

This is where you come to life, but in a controlled way. Rather than talking too much, not listening to the question and constantly going off at a tangent, your answer will be energised, but also focused. Answer clearly, audibly, with evident interest in the question, and be confident that as a result of your preparation your answer is going in the right direction.

CHAPTER SIX

Getting into the right frame of mind

THIS CHAPTER LOOKS AT:

- Trusting in your material
- Working on your mindset
- How not to get in the way of your own goals
- Advice for introverts and extroverts

TRUSTING IN WHAT YOU KNOW

The things you are most worried about the night before an interview may not be the most important problems. You worry about having the right skills and experience, but if you didn't, you wouldn't have got this far. You worry about being up to the job, despite your solid experience. You worry about the questions, knowing that most are predictable. Trust in what you know, and trust in what you have done.

If you're reading a book like this you probably have some ideas about what you'll be talking about at interview, and you may know how to do the right research. You may however wonder how you transform a good interview into a great one. The big issue then is not content, but packaging: *how* you get your evidence across. This means thinking less in intellectual terms (knowledge, facts, information) and more in terms of personal impact (mood, rapport, interaction) – how you will *be* at interview.

GETTING YOUR HEAD IN THE RIGHT PLACE

Career coach Stuart McIntosh says: 'If you've got an interview then the job is yours (why interview someone who you believe isn't capable of doing the job?). If you are not invited back or offered the job then something happened at the interview to change the employer's mind.'

In other words, good candidates make sure that they don't talk themselves out of the job.

If you are up for an interview tomorrow it may be glaringly obvious to your friends that you will come home without a job offer, even though they know nothing about the role. If even members of your family know this in advance, the issue is most probably about your frame of mind.

My colleague, JLA's Managing Consultant Gill Best, captures this well:

> What we think influences how we feel, which then influences how we behave. We routinely reflect on past and future events with 'self-talk'; that voice in our head that is often our worst critic. We're more than ready to believe it without question, but we don't need to.
>
> Instead of telling yourself what is wrong with you and why you won't land the job, tell yourself what is right with you. Remind yourself what you do well, your achievements and your skills; focus on what you have to offer, and why you will be an asset to the company.
>
> Our self-talk and feelings are much more malleable than we recognise. Need a confidence boost? Borrow one from the past. Think of a time you felt really confident then imagine you are back in that place and remember what you saw, heard and how you felt. Can't remember a time? Just imagine

what it would be like. Or look at a photograph of a happy time – and pay attention to how you feel as a result. Do everything you can to *feel* good about the coming interview.

There are two ground rules here:

1   Thinking about your mindset is *not* an excuse for failing to do thorough preparation on the role and the organisation – see Chapter 7.

2   Look seriously at the way that being nervous gets in the way of a solid interview – see Chapter 5.

YOUR TELL-TALE HEART

When you have an interview coming up, look at the way you talk about it. The language you use gives away your underlying approach:

WHAT YOU SAY	WHAT THIS PROBABLY MEANS
'I will see what they ask me'	I will wing it – no point doing that much preparation.
'There's not much more I can do'	I've focused on content and haven't thought very much about the way I appear and sound.
'I am what I am'	I find it too threatening to think about things I do which put people off or get in the way of good answers.
'My memory lets me down'	I haven't bothered to find memory tricks and techniques that work for me personally.
'I get so nervous I let myself down'	I am uniquely immune to relaxation techniques.

▶

WHAT YOU SAY	WHAT THIS PROBABLY MEANS
'It's a lottery'	The outcome of this interview has little to do with me.
'I don't interview well'	I am frightened of making even small changes to my interview technique.
'It's only an interview'	I don't really want to think about it.
'I've been to hundreds of interviews before'	I am going to pretend that there is nothing I can do better.
'I'll never be the strongest candidate'	I would rather worry about perfection than put my focus on being good enough.
'Interviews always go wrong for me'	I would rather put my attention on past problems than the things that went well.
'You can't teach an old dog new tricks'	I put my creativity and energy into avoiding change.

NOT GETTING IN THE WAY OF YOURSELF

Many of the above statements are self-justifying and self-fulfilling. They set limits on what you can do. It's all too easy to take a jaded view about positive thinking, especially in a tough market; telling yourself you are a winner will not guarantee a job offer – an interview isn't *just* about boundless confidence. But confidence does matter – Chapter 10 shows how candidates who are open and positive make a better initial impact.

A big part of confidence is learning how to achieve your goals without getting in your own way. Self-limiting descriptions do exactly this. They say 'I can't ...' when 'I might ...' is perfectly possible. They say 'I never achieve X' when the truth is often 'in the right circumstances I can achieve XXX'.

What this really shows is that we avoid thinking about how we do things. Either that, or we believe we need to change everything. You don't, of course. This is equally true about workplace performance or being a better parent or partner. You just need to learn from experiences, work hard on new approaches, and do your best to make small changes to the things that matter most.

The first big obstacle is *believing you aren't going to get the job*. It's the perfect, self-fulfilling prophecy. So, part of the work you do before an interview is staying positive. This does not mean believing you're invincible or you can do anything – it's simply recognising that you're already close to a job offer and therefore are beginning from a position of strength.

What do you normally say about the experience of being interviewed? Take a friend out for coffee (the same friend whose ear you bend before and after interviews). Ask for feedback about the words you normally use – how have you described yourself, the event, the interviewer? Write the phrases down, and then use highlighter pens in two different colours to categorise them into 'anti' and 'pro':

ANTI – where you said negative things about the process or those interviewing you, or negative things about yourself.

PRO – where you described things that went well, including the relationship in the room, your preparation, and the questions you answered.

Naturally, the 'anti' list is *much* more fun and emotionally rewarding to talk about. This is interview as melodrama, with goodies and baddies, intrigue and disaster. Good entertaining stuff, so get that out of the way first. Over your second cup of coffee, talk about (and add to) the 'pro' list. This area of reflection is more likely to help things go differently.

GOING TO INTERVIEWS 'FOR THE PRACTICE'

You may be planning to apply for a job you don't really want. You say you're applying for interview practice, or 'testing the water'. You could do the job in your sleep, but it would do your ego good to be offered it anyway so you could decline gracefully.

Take some hard advice on this one. Don't do it. The chances are that you will get a rejection, either because of the randomness of selection, or more probably your evident lack of enthusiasm. What you won't be prepared for is the impact of being rejected – 'no' will be just as off-putting here as a 'no' at any stage in the job search process. You've applied for a role that repeats past experience or would be a drop in status, and you didn't even get short listed. What did you expect that to do for your self-confidence? Find opportunities to practise outside the decision-making process.

FEEL IT, SAY IT, SHOW IT – ADVICE FOR INTROVERTS

In an August 2010 survey, the website Gumtree asked employers what qualities they looked for in new staff. Sixty-five per cent rated relevant experience, with higher ratings given to 'skills and competencies', but a substantial 91 per cent rated 'attitude' as the most important factor.

At the beginning of an interview, introverts often send out weaker signals about being confident and personable, and it takes them longer than extroverts to establish relationships. Introverts tend to be more reflective before speaking, and selectors often say introverts often appear to lack enthusiasm, either about the job or their work history. Some introverts are more reluctant to disclose information, and because they reflect when dealing with detailed questions, they can 'close down', which makes them sound detached; the interviewer's snap reaction is often 'seems uninterested – not sure if he wants the job'.

Quieter people need to do a lot more in terms of looking and sounding excited about the role. The good news for introverts is that this is about behaviours you can manage and language you can consciously adopt. Practise using phrases that convey energy: 'I am excited about this ... What really fires me up ... I just love ...'. Learn to sound as if you mean it. Practise your stories not just for plot but for engagement (see also Chapter 13 on getting your story across) – create a picture of a specific occasion when you did something important.

Get someone who knows you well to give you feedback on positive body language so it all fits together. You don't have to transform yourself into the life and soul of the party, simply show what you are like on a good day.

STEP BACK A LITTLE – ADVICE FOR EXTROVERTS

Extroverts are often more comfortable talking about themselves and naturally open up quickly, tell animated stories and 'broadcast' energy, so as a result they often have a headstart at interview. Sometimes this appearance is overwhelming for the quieter interviewer and can easily be misread as over-confidence or someone who is likely to be too loud or too dominant in the workplace.

Introverts are inclined to think and then speak, whereas extroverts often don't know what they think until they say it out loud, so it pays to be slightly more thoughtful about your answers rather than jumping in with the first thing you think of. Don't overwhelm the interviewer by being 'in your face' – try to be in sync. Gill Best advises 'match your energy level to the energy in the room'.

PLAYING THE INTERVIEW GAME BY THE PROPER RULES

An interview is not an exam paper with right and wrong answers – an idea we reinforce by talking about 'homework' and 'predicting questions'. Careers expert Claire Coldwell says: 'An interview is not really a "test" – interviewers are genuinely seeking to have a relaxed and open enough dialogue to get closer to that decision about whether the person sitting in front of them can solve their vacancy problem. So that means engaging with the process, doing proper research and preparation and thinking hard about what the interviewer might need to know. Spending a day interviewing can be hard work, and it's much easier if someone is engaged in the process!' Be flexible: attune yourself carefully to the interviewer's needs in terms of content and communication style.

An interview is in fact a kind of half-understood game, where the winner walks away with the prize, while fellow contestants scratch their heads because they were playing by different rules. This game is also an audition, so it helps to get in role. Some candidates have achieved great results by imagining they are a colleague they admire or a particular film star. If it helps reveal a stronger version of you, it's an appropriate form of preparation.

When career coaches and recruitment consultants send clients off to job interviews they often know in advance who will get an offer and who won't. The reason is rarely about experience, skills or knowledge. It's about the intangibles – the initial impression you make, the way you start talking, your ability to establish relationships and look confident even if your heart is racing.

Having some influence over this 'chemistry' means learning to see yourself as others see you. But there's no point doing this just to beat yourself up, reinforcing the idea 'I don't interview well'. Awareness must lead to change – not total transformation or 'faking it', but learning to project the best version of you, time after time. Chapter 8 recommends a range of positive outcomes you can achieve from using video, but you can also get good feedback by talking to a friend or colleague who is capable of telling you, objectively, what you do well, and what needs improving. Ask specifically about the energy levels in your answers. Do you sound positive, enthusiastic and motivated by what you are talking about? Conveying energy in the interview room communicates real interest in the job, but also shows you'll be an enthusiastic member of the team.

CHAPTER SEVEN

How much preparation is enough?

THIS CHAPTER HELPS YOU TO THINK ABOUT:

- Why we give lip service to interview preparation
- The ways we fail to interrogate job information properly
- Looking at all the dimensions of interview preparation
- Anticipating the interviewer checklist

THE STANDARD APPROACH

Strangely enough, even though interview advice *always* talks about preparation, candidates don't really believe in it. How do we know? Every day employers see candidates who have no idea about the role, the organisation, haven't thought about the questions that might be asked, and have given very little consideration to what questions they might ask themselves. As an approach it's very popular, as evidenced by the interview stage of *The Apprentice* where there is always someone who appears to know nothing at all about the organisation they hope to join.

Ways of *pretending* that you have done the right kind of preparation include:

1   just looking at the job description (rather than finding out background details about the job);

2   focusing only on those topic areas where you have pre-prepared answers, and using those answers even when they don't fit the question;

3   assuming that the questions will be obvious (rather than working out what they will actually be);

4   vaguely remembering general interview tips (rather than thinking about this specific interview).

So, the standard approach nods to preparation but in fact puts it on a low footing. There's a good analogy in what we know about the environment and global warming. Today's Xbox generation claims to have a high awareness of green issues, but when tested the actual knowledge of teenagers is often worse than their parents. A large gulf may exist between what we believe we know, and reality.

If someone told you that the next decade of your career depended on a half-hour conversation with your boss tomorrow morning, you'd prepare for it well enough. You'd probably revisit your successes and failures over the last year, think about ways of presenting your work history in the best light, and no doubt you would ask around to find out what your boss is most enthusiastic about right now. You would not wing it.

A new job will impact on the next ten years of your working life and reshape your CV, so why would you consider a conversation about getting it a trivial event? Interviews matter, and the only way to ensure success is proper, focused preparation.

'ONE-SHEET MATCHING'

Stage one of your preparation is to dig quickly into whatever information you can find out about the role itself. A note of caution is required here. You can't trust job descriptions. Ask candidates or recruiters alike – it is universally acknowledged that they are only a partial picture, often out of date, and sometimes pure fiction.

Take an A4 sheet of paper and draw a line down the middle. In the left-hand column write down all the items you believe an employer is looking for. That means going way, way beyond the job description – look at clues in the job advertisement, from any of the documents used in the selection process, from your organisational research, and seek additional tips from industry contacts. You are after the complete shopping list, including the things you get from reading between the lines, remembering that attitude and personality also matter. For example, if the job ad says 'we are a rapidly growing and enthusiastic team' it is clear that the employer wants to see ambition combined with visible enthusiasm. Where a job calls for 'good communication skills' show this in the interview, but also have some good examples to hand. If the job is a business development role with a 'long established manufacturer' and 'stable organisation', you probably need to show personal drive and a sensitive understanding of organisational culture. Try, if you can, to distinguish between the items your potential employer must have and the ones that are simply preferred.

The right-hand column is your space to write down your matching evidence. Use bullet points, but write it all down, even though you think you know it, because the more you instruct your memory to behave itself now, the less you will have to use it in the interview room itself.

Work out the employer's shopping list and you will work out about 80 per cent of the questions that will come up. Prepare for each question and each topic as if that question alone will decide whether you get the job.

HOW MUCH IS ENOUGH?

That's a very reasonable question, since you could spend forever preparing for an interview, or spend too much time preparing the wrong things. There are four big ticket items in your preparation: Organisation, Role, People and Yourself (preparing yourself is a big topic, which Chapter 8 explores in considerable detail).

Organisation

The organisation is not your specialist *Mastermind* subject, but doing more homework than the average candidate really shows that you are interested in this role, rather than just in need of a job. However, all your research needs to be applied. I have known candidates who could talk about an organisation down to the last statistical detail, but showed no ability at all to match themselves to the role.

Career coach Sheryl Spanier writes: 'My experience is that it is critical that the candidate has a real interest in and excitement in the position ... and shows it. Demonstrate reflection and insight about the needs of the organization and ways you can contribute. Too often this kind of energy is lacking, especially when the candidate thinks they should not look too "hungry". The irony is that employers really want to hire people who really want to work for them.'

Your background research will not be a complete overview (you're not buying the company), but information which fits one of the following three categories: (1) you look stupid if you don't know; (2) it shows you understand how the job contributes to a bigger picture; (3) it gives you an opportunity to shine.

Don't leave all your research until the night before the interview. Wherever possible, talk to people who can fill some of the gaps – ideally those who have worked in the organisation recently. Undertake about an hour's Internet research on the organisation before any interview. Interrogate the organisation's website, but also Google the company name and scroll down beyond the first 10 hits. You should have a clear sense of what kind of organisation it is, how long it has been around, what it makes or delivers, its culture, and who the key players are.

Add to that basic mix anything you can find about past successes and future plans. Often the 'Press Releases' or 'News' buttons on the website will reveal press headlines or PR campaigns. Anything positive provides good interview material – new products, awards, contracts won, innovations, new people hired, celebrities who have some connection with the business. 'Match your approach to the company's values', advises outplacement specialist Isabel Chadwick. 'If they talk about customer focus and being accountable then emphasise how you have focused on these in previous roles.'

It's best not to mention information which the organisation may consider not entirely in the public domain ('a contact tells me that your sales figures are down this quarter') or negative results (product recalls, falling share price). Imagine a good friend says 'Why do you want to work *there*?' What could you say about the way the organisation matches what you are looking for? Would you sound as if you know enough to decide whether to take the job?

Zena Everett ran a recruitment business before retraining as a career management specialist. Her advice is to show you understand the big picture: 'It is particularly important for managers to show that they are aware how their role contributes more broadly to the department and organisation they work in. When describing past successes always try to include a "big" outcome, rather than just solving problems or dealing with issues.'

Role

Much of this has already been covered in the 'One-sheet matching' section, but there is more to consider. Documents describing roles tend to list *all* the qualities considered vital in the ideal candidate. Don't be put off by that – employers usually get only 60–70 per cent of what they are looking for. The bigger problem, however, is that it can be a very long list. Some candidates have to deal with lists of up to 30 competencies, and then discover that only a fraction of them are actually discussed at interview.

Decoding jobs requires a certain kind of cynicism. Just as organisations make huge claims about their values and mission statement and then act somewhat differently, jobs are also overstated or oversold. So, in a sense, what you are doing is learning to tell the difference between what the employer says it wants and the true reason a job is available. Sometimes you have to rely on instinct to work out what an employer really wants, but it's better to do your research and be sure.

What job descriptions rarely tell you is the answer to four key questions:

1   **What's the history?** Is this a new role – if so, why? If not, what happened to the last post holder?

2   **From the long list of competencies, *what matters most?*** In other words, what items on the list are really important, and what are just padding to make the job description look complete?

3   **How is the job likely to change?** This tells you something about how quickly the goalposts normally move.

4   **What does winning look like?** You won't be expected to deliver on everything, so what things will you need to concentrate on for this appointment to be considered a success?

Finding the answers to these questions requires the kind of

spadework that marks out the above average candidate. You may get some details from a recruitment consultant, and sometimes you are invited to talk the role through with the organisation or the current post holder or manager before interview.

Far more often you will need to ask around, beginning with anyone you know who works at or near this organisation. When you know the answers to the above four questions, pack them into your key messages (see Chapter 12).

Preparing for the role also means preparing good questions to ask at the end of the interview. Avoid questions which are naive (asking obvious questions about the job) or misplaced (this is the wrong time to talk about salary or benefits). Use at least one well-researched question about the organisation during small talk, and one or two detailed ones at the end of the interview (see Chapter 12).

People

It's a perfectly reasonable request to say 'Who will be inter-viewing me, and what are their responsibilities?' Again, it shows a bit of spark. When phoning you can also check on how names are pronounced. Research these individuals using the company's website but also external sources such as LinkedIn.

Establish their seniority and their experience, but focus on their respective roles in the organisation, and ask yourself where each person's focus will be. A line manager, for example, may have problems that need sorting out immediately, but a more senior executive may be more interested in your long-term potential.

Career management consultant Ruth Winden advises: 'Research interviewers' backgrounds, and then weave relevant information into the interview sparingly and at the right moment. Look for experiences in common, such as school, university, alumni, employers, countries worked in, contacts, associations. Not many job seekers search for this type of information, so it's easy to stand out from the crowd. Looking at pictures of interviewers prior to the meeting will calm your nerves and get around the challenge of having to remember names when you are being interviewed by several people at once.'

DECODING THE INTERVIEWER CHECKLIST

Although an interview may be a high-adrenaline experience for you, it's routine for the interviewer. They have a job to do, and that includes obtaining information which matches their checklist. That checklist may be written out in the interviewer's paperwork, or may just be in the interviewer's head. Either way, you need to work out in advance what points are covered and have your evidence at your fingertips (see 'one-sheet matching' earlier in this chapter).

If you know that a broad range of skills will be discussed, you reduce your chances by talking too long about just one skill. Less assured candidates say too much in the early part of the interview and this compresses their opportunities later. Early on, keep your answers short and focused, because then you let the interviewer choose between probing what you have just said or moving on to the next topic.

And what if the interviewer's questions appear under-prepared and unrelated to any clear checklist? Offer your best mix of evidence, and work hard on conveying the right 'fit' (because if an interviewer is vague on skills their focus is usually on personality issues). However, it's a good idea part way through the interview to re-establish terms by asking a question like 'I'd be interested to know what skills and qualities you expect to see in a top performer in this job.'

CHAPTER EIGHT

How do I prepare *myself*?

THIS CHAPTER LOOKS AT:

- Your interview insurance policy
- Managing the things under your control
- Understanding 'the look'
- Professional behaviours
- Getting ready for your screen test

INSURANCE

Readers of interview books understandably complain if advice seems obvious, but the number of people who fail to put the basics into practice is considerable. So, the basics are worth repeating, if only because they provide valuable insurance against things going wrong – at least the things within your control.

Any of the following could ruin your day if you fail to anticipate them:

1   Double check the interview location. Use a map as well as your satnav, and ring in advance if you are not sure about which building or entrance you go to.

2   Plan your journey meticulously – take an earlier train than you need to or allow time for traffic. Check where and

how to park: if it's a pay and display system, take enough change to pay for an hour more than you need in case things over-run (an extended interview is a strong buying signal, so don't wreck it by having to rush out).

3 Get a good night's sleep. Going into an assessment in a haze of sleep deprivation and caffeine indulgence is no way to start.

4 Take any documents you will need during the interview process, which will include organisational and job information and a copy of the exact version of the CV and cover letter you used to get short listed. Take a small pad and paper too.

5 Get the timing right. Showing up late signals poor commitment, more than ten minutes early shows desperation. Ten minutes is plenty of time to settle down and chat with reception staff (they may be asked how you came across).

6 Declutter – leave your coat, umbrella and bag in reception. Just take in a slim folder containing the documents you need, and you will look like an employee rather than a visitor.

7 Switch your phone off as you arrive. No distractions.

'THE LOOK'

Take advice from people who just know what makes people look good and look right. Try your outfit on in front of a mirror (or a good friend). The right question is not 'Do I look good?' but 'What picture is presented here?' We remember images far more clearly than words. Remember that image and dress sense change across organisations and cultures. Don't guess or assume, find out.

If you don't 'get' the whole image thing, put yourself in the hands of someone who does. This needn't cost you a fortune. Book advice is useful, but no match for trying things on with the help of someone with good instincts. Often it's a question of buying clothes that look classically smart in an understated kind of way. Men in particular seem to err when matching patterns and colours and some fail consistently in the art of tying a tie so that the knot sits tightly under the chin. Chaps, if you have doubts about buying an outfit, often the best combination of suit, tie and shirt is the one on the model in the shop.

Take advice (see Mary Spillane's books) – suits should be current but not too trendy, avoid perfume, and shoes should match the quality of your suit. The right interview outfit shows a candidate is professional, organised and focused; sloppy dress is usually taken as an indication of poor attention to detail, a dated or worn-out outfit a sign that you're out of touch with the workplace.

Wear clothes that are just slightly smarter than those worn in the workplace, and choose something slightly conservative such as a well-fitting suit in a solid, dark colour. Playing safe and looking like you're in business 'uniform' means that your outfit is quickly forgotten.

Dress the part, but don't overdo it – your clothes shouldn't be more interesting than you. A good benchmark is what business people wear for TV interviews – something instantly recognisable as smart and business-like allows the viewer to focus quickly on the words being spoken. Remember the last time that you saw a TV interviewee wearing over-bright colours or a loud tie? You formed an immediate impression, but did you remember what was said? Women should avoid large, distracting jewellery, men should definitely save gimmicky socks and wacky ties for another occasion.

Choose something you are comfortable in rather than something brand new that still feels strange – particularly true of shoes. Put on interview clothes the day before the interview and practise sitting down in them, otherwise you will always look and feel like the new kid who hasn't got used to the school uniform. Not only that, but if there are problems (shoes that squeak, clothes that don't look right when you sit down) you will discover the problem in good time. Similarly, if you change your hairstyle the day before a job interview you will not feel at ease.

Recruitment specialist Graeme Dixon of Cast Consulting writes: 'If in doubt always dress formally with gentlemen wearing a professional tie. Clean, shiny shoes are a must. If the company has a dress-down policy ask the interviewer what you should wear, but even if it is an informal dress culture your clothes should still be clean and well-pressed, and other aspects including hair and jewellery not distracting – informal does not mean scruffy. It is essential a candidate looks as if they could walk straight into the job. Going into an interview in a pinstripe suit when the interviewers are in jeans will not give the right impression.'

PROFESSIONAL BEHAVIOURS

An organisation picks up evidence about you well before you open your mouth. How you arrive, for example – quiet and professional, or in a flurry of anxiety about late running trains. Do you come in carrying all kinds of bags as if you're half way through a shopping trip?

Then, of course, you speak. As soon as you arrive, your behaviour is monitored, including the first words you say to the reception staff. 'The interview starts the moment you arrive on a client's premises', writes career coach Beverley Grant. 'When I recruited employees for a large IT company I often asked the staff on reception or any other employees who came into contact with the candidates what their impression was because when not in the formal interview people can sometimes behave differently.'

'Practise your smile', advises Kathryn Jackson, author of *How to Keep Your Cool if You Lose Your Job*. 'If you're not confident at meeting people for the first time (or you know it takes you a little time to warm up), practise making eye contact and smiling at everybody you meet on the street (bus drivers, supermarket scanners, doormen, you name it ... smile at them). You might worry that they will think you're nuts, but when they start smiling back at you then you can feel more confident that you've become able to make a good first impression to others.'

Language is a particularly powerful indicator – your tone, delivery and the choice of words are very much part of the audition. Remember that all the time your interviewer is transposing you into a different context and wondering whether you will be the right person. Think carefully about the language you use to describe difficult experiences, particularly those involving stress or conflict.

Always, always, avoid criticism of former bosses, employers or customers. Avoid emotive language unless it's positive: enthusiasm, yes; bitterness, no. Be very careful in the words you use to describe areas of difference – there is a big variation between 'we saw the world differently' and 'he was a complete idiot'.

'Bad' language ranges from swearing (don't do it, even if the interviewer does) through to inappropriate friendliness – calling the interviewer 'mate' or 'sweetheart' are characteristics which have got candidates a 'no' letter. Pulling faces, extreme gestures, making noises – these are forms of communication which can be instantly off-putting.

Graeme Dixon writes: 'When a candidate enters a room for an interview I always suggest a genuine smile and look at each of the people in the room, thanking them for seeing you. Wait to be asked to sit down and when asked how your journey was reply in a positive way. It is essential to maintain a positive impression. Complaining about the traffic is not the best start to an important interview. Once you have sat down, come out with a positive one-liner, like "I have to say how much I am looking forward to this meeting as it is an exciting opportunity." It also allows the interviewer a natural and positive starting point.'

As soon as you leave the room, an interviewer naturally runs a mental 'movie' of what you have said and done. So, when you are in the interview room, even if it is informal and just the two of you in the room, imagine that movie being recorded, and then played back on a large screen in your city centre in front of an audience that is going to give you a YES or a NO card simply on the grounds of personality. What do you say, entirely independent of content, which shouts out 'NO'? Get feedback on that well before you go anywhere near an organisational decision maker.

Think about getting in and out of an interview room. This isn't as strange as it sounds. When we are nervous, hands and feet go in unexpected directions, and you may crash into furniture or drop papers. If you were walking out onstage where there were steps, chairs and a lectern to fall over, you'd practise. You can't physically practise in the interview room, but you can remember to pause and plan. Stand in the doorway and look at the room, and *think* about how you are going to get into the interview seat without difficulty (another reason why it's a good idea to leave your bag and coat in reception).

SCREEN TEST

Imagine that the next few minutes are going to be like a screen test for a part you are going to have to play for a long time. Just as a director watches a screen test of an actor trying on a role, an interviewer is wondering whether you can play the part. That's why an important unstated part of the interview is observing professional behaviours.

This begins with image, body language, and instant impact, but extends to a range of behaviours which matter in this particular workplace – clarity and tone of voice for a call centre job; the way you inform, direct and delegate as a manager; the ability to use diplomatic or inclusive language in sensitive contexts. These behaviours are also partly measured by the way you tune into the social niceties of the interview. The interviewer is trying to get a clear picture of what you will be like in the job – for example, imagining how you would appear to senior colleagues.

Research studies (see Michael Watkins' *The First 90 Days*, Harvard Business School Press, 2003) suggest that anything up to 50 per cent of external appointments fail to achieve the desired results. So a big factor for any recruiter is looking good, particularly when they take the risk of choosing an external candidate. The person offering you the job will feel under considerable scrutiny the first time you are introduced to the MD or the team. Will you look and sound like a good hiring decision?

CLOSE THE FEEDBACK LOOP

The difficulty for some is that they never see themselves the way others do, and are unaware of their impact. Since these people are often the last to 'get it', the best safety mechanism is for everyone, no matter how brilliantly you think you interview, to triangulate their perspective. Here are the three vital steps:

1   **Self:** Write down how you think you come across, how you communicate, what your style is, the things you see that help your performance, and the things that get in the way.

2   **Coach:** Get someone else to give you a short mock interview and get some honest feedback before telling them the list you came up with in (1). You may be surprised by what goes well, and what doesn't. Ask for tough love, not unconditional affirmation.

3   **Video:** Get someone to video your performance. Watch it several times, on your own and with a colleague. Now

turn the picture off and listen to the soundtrack – are you clear, interesting, with answers the right length? Now – most importantly – watch it again *with the sound off.* What are you communicating without words?

GETTING THE RIGHT ADVICE

Because interviews occur so widely it shouldn't be hard, by asking around, to get advice from someone who has experience of conducting them. However, do be aware that many general managers overrate their interviewing skills – try to find someone with an HR or recruitment background who can put you through a professionally structured interview, probing your CV and your answers in depth. You don't want someone who last interviewed in 1985, or someone who tells you you're wonderful and shouldn't change a thing.

CHAPTER NINE

I have to make a presentation …

THIS CHAPTER LOOKS AT:

- What (usually) leads to an undercharged performance
- The way a presentation is a gift opportunity
- Getting under the skin of the task
- PowerPoint tips – working without notes
- Tuning your presentation into the big '90-day question'

THE BIG HURDLE

Some employers will ask you to make a short presentation, usually immediately before an interview. This can seem daunting – you have to communicate on your feet to an audience which is probably going to be critical rather than supportive, and you know that everything you do is being assessed. What's more, a presentation means an audience, which usually indicates at least two people interviewing.

WHAT GOES WRONG

Over the years of fishing for feedback from candidates and interviewers I am pretty sure that if anything is going to go wrong it's probably something from this list:

The 10 most common features of shaky presentations

1 Stilted, under-rehearsed opening.

2 Misunderstanding (and usually, over-complicating) the task.

3 Speaking too quickly, trying to cram in 50 ideas into 5 minutes on the assumption that some of it might stick.

4 Having too much material so you overrun and have to be stopped part-way through your flow.

5 Putting far too many long sentences on each PowerPoint slide, and reading them all out.

6 Being wooden, sounding uncomfortable, failing to engage with the audience.

7 Failing to leave some questions open so that you have a good footing to start the interview.

8 Failing to establish eye contact with anyone in the room.

9 Striking the wrong balance in answers to the 90-day question (see below).

10 A flat ending that sounds as if you're not sure whether you're finished or not.

MAKING MOVIES

A presentation is a gift. A large part of the interview process is about getting a movie running in the interviewer's head which shows you doing the job. While it may take half an interview to get that picture across, a presentation can do it in a couple of minutes. Why? Because it immediately answers questions like 'Will this person be credible addressing the Board?' ... 'How will she come across in a heads of department meeting?' ... 'Can we be confident of his ability to address the public?'

Look at any movie showcasing a major star, and watch the first 60 seconds that actor is on screen. In those seconds as a character is established you often decide whether it's going to be a good film or not. Presentations have the same power to intensify first impressions, so the first part of your presentation is not your script, but the immediate impact you make just by standing up. Work hard on your 'look' (see Chapter 8), and get some feedback. When you walk in and begin presenting, how well does the person on show match the person presented on paper? Career coach Bernard Pearce says 'Organisations form an opinion of you long before they see you, so be who they are hoping you will be!'

THE TASK

Normally employers will give you presentation topics in advance, but most are predictable – however it's dressed up, the presentation topic is usually, in essence, 'show us how well you understand what we're trying to do, and tell us how you will make an impact'.

Think carefully about what the employer really expects you to deliver. Most candidates try to fit in too much. You will probably spend anything between two to four minutes talking about each PowerPoint slide, so don't expect to get through more than four to five slides in a 10-minute presentation – you will probably be stopped at the time limit, cutting out your closing points. Make sure slides are not over-stuffed with text. Limit yourself to three or four punchy bullet points you can expand upon. If you will be using PowerPoint, do check what practical arrangements will be in place – email your presentation in advance (take a back-up on data stick), and enquire tactfully if the equipment will already be set up and tested before you use it.

The main reason to welcome a presentation is that it gives you a great opportunity to show how you can analyse an organisation and its problems, even for a relatively junior job. Rather than repeating random facts, try to paint the big picture. This requires care, because you can easily sound glib or lacking in research.

A presentation will often work around three key stages:

1   **Analysis** – saying briefly what you see and understand. The more this sounds like a 'helicopter view' the better.

2   **Making connections** – drawing different pieces of evidence together, including perspectives from outside the organisation, and possibly your own experience, too.

3   Suggested **actions** – clear recommendations. These will inevitably be slightly cautious because you would of course need more detail before implementation.

REHEARSE, REHEARSE

The good news is that performance anxiety lessens the more you do something. Your brain starts to recognise contexts and starts to say 'This is OK, I have been here before.' Interestingly, this is equally true for rehearsal as it is for actual performance, and even works with visualised scenarios. So the act of imagining yourself doing well in a presentation, thinking through the positive phrases you will use, starts to build a kind of mock memory of success.

The problem is that few people actually rehearse interviews or presentations. They say 'I guess I will talk about ...' or 'My answer will be something along the lines of ...', when what they actually need to do is to answer real interview questions and pitch actual presentations. Find people who have some experience of conducting interviews and get them to hear what you have to say, and then probe you on the points you make. Tell them the questions you are most worried about, and then answer them, for real, using exactly the words you would use in an interview. So not 'I will probably say ...' but 'I did ...'.

SPEAKING FROM NOTES

Very few people can trust themselves to speak without notes, but over-reliance on notes almost guarantees a wooden performance. In any case, most people find it difficult to read text while they are talking to an audience. What's more, holding papers or cards in your hand and looking down at them requires you to hunch your shoulders and stoop slightly, which broadcasts timidity and takes your focus off building rapport with the audience.

There are several strategies to get past this. The first is mandatory, and one you should never ignore: learn the beginning and the end of your talk by heart, so you can deliver these segments without looking down at your notes or up at a screen. The beginning and the end are what will be remembered most, so getting those right matters. A clear, strong, beginning boosts your confidence, and a well-crafted ending to a presentation puts the start of your interview on a high note. *Plan the actual words* – whether this is a conclusion, a question, a challenge, or an invitation: 'I'd be happy to provide further details during our conversation today.'

Next, think about how you will deliver the rest of your material with minimum reference to notes. It helps to design slides which prompt you. *Never* read slides out, always paraphrase, or say something tangential to the material. For example, if your slide says 'There are three main ways forward for this organisation' you've robbed yourself of a great line. Better to have a short statement ('Strategies for success') or a question ('Is there a way forward?'), and then your slide has a dual function – it grabs attention, and prompts your next words.

As you get more experienced you will see that short on-screen phrases work best, especially if they get your audience thinking. Imagine a slide which shows an image of an hourglass and says '10 minutes = £200'. You've given your audience a puzzle and if you then explain (every 10 minutes spent with a customer costs £200), you've caught their attention a second time. Use on-screen material to tantalise, tempt, draw people in, rather than telling them the whole story. Try cutting down each bullet point to one or two words.

CARTOON SHEET

If the slide itself doesn't give you a strong enough steer in terms of script, try not to fall back on prompt cards. It's very hard indeed to read text while you are speaking – your attention is easily distracted if you lose your place, and your gaze is locked down onto your document. If you rely on written notes you need to find your place, remember what the words meant, and then turn them into spoken phrases.

What works much better is to draw a sequence of symbols or cartoons which summarise your presentation. Divide up a page into squares laid out like a comic book. For each segment, each example or argument, draw a picture or a symbol, which you will find much easier to take in at a glance. For example, if I want to remember that I have to say that 'this organisation will get better results if it encourages staff to be more creative and more flexible', draw a light bulb (idea) over a wavy line (flexibility), next to the organisation's initials. Instead of writing 'Three Steps To Motivating Teams' draw a staircase of three steps leading to smiling faces. You get the idea. Put all the images you need for your talk on one piece of card and keep it just in sight, and your presenting style, with a bit of rehearsal, will be transformed.

THE '90-DAY QUESTION'

'What do you hope to achieve in your first three months?' is a question you might be asked at interview, and your presentation may be about ideas you can bring to the role. In a way, *every* presentation is about this topic. Long-term success will often be based on your visibility within that three-month window, and your interviewer is trying to work out what you will look like in the role and what impact you might make.

Take this seriously, because (apart from being an audition for the kind of role you will have to undertake) that's what the presentation is about – whether you 'get' the needs underlying the role, and whether you can deliver.

Answering the '90-day question' takes a lot of thinking. If you are asked about changes or improvements you would make, be careful. Some candidates say 'I wouldn't make any changes until I had learned a lot more about the organisation and consulted with my colleagues.' That answer is not only predictable but a little too safe for most jobs.

At the other end of the spectrum is the kind of candidate who tells the organisation every mistake it's making and offers to give things a pretty big shake-up – usually enough to put the interviewers' backs up.

How far you emphasise caution or suggest specific changes depends on the nature of the role, but the best answers take a middle ground between the two which effectively says 'Yes, I will learn and listen, but I will also get on with things.'

It's unwise to be deeply critical of the organisation – the system you are trashing could be the brainchild of one of the people in the room. Better approaches say 'this is the approach I would take ...', 'here's something I have tried elsewhere which I believe could help you'. If you have a proposed strategy, present it as a suggestion open to questions rather than the only way of doing things. If the big strategy is beyond your grasp without knowing a lot more about the organisation, offer some quick wins – short-term results that can be obtained at minimal cost without treading on anyone's toes.

CHAPTER TEN

How do I manage the opening moments?

THIS CHAPTER LOOKS AT:

- The critical opening moments
- First impressions – do they count all that much?
- What kind of decision does an interviewer make?
- How do you manage the initial minutes of the interview?

THE FIRST FEW SECONDS

It is Christmas morning on the battlefield. Two men approach each other in no man's land. They watch each other with great care, watching for sudden movement, for a weapon, for a signal for a sniper's shot. Eyes dart constantly from one hand to the other, to the face, the eyes.

One man speaks, and even though the other soldier does not understand the words, in his fear he listens carefully to the tone, the sounds of reassurance. Carefully, slowly, gifts are offered, some chocolate, some Schnapps. As the items are slowly exchanged, this time they look only at each other's faces, which very slowly break into smiles.

A familiar wartime scene, which teaches us a great deal about the opening moments of an encounter where two human beings don't trust each other and have reasons to be fearful. Without over-dramatising the much safer environment of the job interview, it is helpful to think about times when body language, movement, words and tone of voice make all the difference.

Be aware what your brain is doing in the opening moments of an interview. It is engaging all the 'fight or flight' mechanisms of your ancestors, working out whether this is a safe place to be, whether to be cautiously defensive, outright aggressive, or simply to sprint out of the door. Let's face it, we've all been in situations where we have been tempted to do at least one of these.

This is why the opening moments of a job interview are the most important. You are at your most uncertain and your most vulnerable at exactly the same time as the interviewer is forming an initial view.

OPENING MOMENTS – FOLKLORE AND REALITY

Many career books and websites tell you that a complete, decisive hiring decision is made in the first few seconds of an interview. Look further and you will see there is no scientific research to back up this claim. Think about it – if an employer had all the information they needed in a minute or so, interviews would end at that point. Interview time is expensive for employers, and if they could get the right result by the work equivalent of speed dating, they would.

The most thorough interviews do not guarantee a perfect outcome, even when backed up with tests and other tools. So we live in an odd world where employers claim to be able to spot the ideal candidate in 10 seconds, yet also admit that they frequently hire the wrong person or fail to spot talent.

What seems true is that we form initial impressions which, for a short while, take a grip on our decision making. Malcolm Gladwell's book *Blink* (2005) argues that we make snap, unconscious judgements which rely 'on the thinnest slices of experience' every time we encounter a new person, situation or idea.

One of the first things we do as babies is to learn to read faces quickly, working out if this is someone we recognise and find friendly. We can apparently spot a smile from 30 metres away.

When our brain 'thin-slices' reality we make instantaneous judgements based on minimal amounts of information. If you're avoiding predators in the wild, it's an instinct that keeps you alive. Today we use the same kind of unconscious mapping in many areas of life, including shopping and dating.

Professor Nalini Ambady researched this effect by asking observers to watch videotapes of lecturers at Harvard University. Presented with a silent 10-second video clip, observers had no difficulty rating the teachers on a 15-point checklist of person-ality traits. When Ambady made the clips even shorter, the ratings were the same.

Ambady compared these findings with evaluations students made after a full semester of classes, and the correlation was astonishing: someone watching a two-second video of a teacher he has never met will reach conclusions about personality very similar to those of a student who has sat in the teacher's class for many lectures.

Additional research undertaken by social psychologist Frank Bernieri required strangers to watch 15-second videos of applicants – knocking on the interview door, entering the room, shaking hands, sitting and being welcomed. These strangers rated the 'handshake clip' using the same criteria used by interviewers who had spent extensive time with these candidates. Once more, against all expectations, the ratings were very similar when looking at 9 out of 11 personality traits.

WHAT IMPACT DO FIRST IMPRESSIONS REALLY HAVE ON INTERVIEWERS?

Extroversion and sociability are the most immediate and obvious aspects of personality, and research shows that we measure these in others quickly and (largely) accurately. Interestingly, we are also more likely to trust instinctive judgements if we feel happy – so an outgoing person who makes the interviewer feel relaxed will always have a headstart. Therefore first impressions are not about the whole picture or about job effectiveness; they are almost entirely about how far someone is personable, friendly and open.

What seems to happen next depends on the interviewer, and is often subject to *confirmation bias* – where we seek out and favour evidence which validates a preconception regardless of whether the information is true. Professionally trained interviewers may seek broader, perhaps even contradictory evidence – if your first impression is not backed up with facts the initial glow may fade.

So, yes, in the first few seconds an interviewer makes some kind of decision, but this is not a hiring decision. It may, however, be a quick answer to the question 'Can I get on with this person?' Gill Best says 'rapport transforms a dry exchange of information into a warm conversation. To develop rapport requires that you focus completely on the other person and respond not only to what is being said but also the way it is being said. Good rapport has a feeling of being in sync, as you will remember from enjoyable conversations you've had in the past. So stop focusing on yourself and focus on the interviewer; they want to have a good experience too.'

MAKING THE OPENING MOMENTS WORK FOR YOU

Psychologists sometimes warn selectors about candidate 'impression management' (as if the interview process was ever about anything else!). From a candidate perspective, *everything* in the hiring process is about impression management – every stage is your opportunity to influence the way someone sees you. If the interviewer has a picture you want to adjust, this should be done openly – 'I expect you're worried about …', or 'You might be assuming that …'.

Although there is no single magic tool that predicts job performance, one of the most reliable is *intelligence*. This isn't about having a bagful of paper qualifications; it's about being smart, interested, focused and curious. This is revealed in the way you reflect on your experience, your 'take' on employer problems, and your questions at the end of the interview.

FIRST IMPRESSION MASTERCLASS

Careers specialist Stuart McIntosh writes that 'at interview there are two key elements – the "non-verbals" (handshake, body language, tone, delivery) and the psychological (confidence, believing you can get the job). Eighty per cent of success at interview relate to these two intertwined factors.'

As we have seen, 'chemistry' starts in the first seconds and there's plenty you can do to make a great impression. Below are some important reminders about first impressions. The first group is for those who are new to the interview process, the second for those who are more experienced at being interviewed but want to improve.

Category 1 – Little interview experience

- Arrive **unflustered** – this generally requires good journey planning. Double check everything.

- What does the interviewer decide about you when you walk in the room? Get your image right – see Chapter 8.

- Prepare for interview **nerves**. Read Chapter 5.

- Be courteous, thank them for inviting you to interview, introduce yourself to each person in the room and wait to be asked to sit down. Remember to also thank them for their time at the end of the interview.

- Communicate the right **attitude**. Do your homework and show real interest in the organisation.

- Use your **body** to communicate attentiveness and energy – sit up straight and lean forward slightly. Pull your shoulders back slightly and breathe from your abdomen – your voice will sound calmer through sounding deeper, and it will help you relax.

- Be **open** and friendly – to everyone, particularly reception staff. Smile every now and again; it won't kill you.

- A firm but not aggressive **handshake** works best if you stand square on to the person shaking your hand and look them in the eye at the same time. Every other variant – limp, damp, fingertips only, over-hearty – puts you on the back foot. Practise!

- Start on a **warm** note. Be prepared to say something relaxed but clear about simple topics like weather and traffic. Ask interested questions about the building or organisation.

- Rehearse out and minimise **verbal tics** used as fillers such as 'you know', 'kind of', 'absolutely', or stock phrases like saying 'What we did was ...' every time.

- Communicate some degree of **confidence** by speaking clearly. Don't 'boom' or over-broadcast. If you are naturally very audible you may need to tone things down, but most people need to make their speaking voice slightly louder than normal. Small talk in the interview room helps you to get a feel for how your voice sounds in that space.

- **Pace** yourself – for most people this means slowing

down slightly so that what you say is clear and sounds thoughtful. Racing to deliver examples usually ends up sounding like a frenetic jumble sale. Speaking *too* slowly makes you sound impossible to motivate.

- Anticipate **gaps and snags**. Think in advance about reasons why an employer might want to withhold a job offer. If there is anything you lack (qualifications, experience, a skill?) think about balancing evidence (e.g. 'I don't hold a management qualification but I have been a manager in a structured environment for 10 years and my achievements include ...').

- **Prepare, prepare, prepare** – not just your narratives (see Chapter 13) but also **your questions** for the end (see Chapter 12). You will always give an impression of confidence if you have clear plans for what you will say.

Category 2 – You can't tell me much about being interviewed but I will read this for interest

- Be **courteous**. Yes, you've been through this a hundred times and the interviewer is half your age, but your readiness to respond openly to the process and observe the social niceties is the first thing that's noticed. Don't be arrogant. If you sound as if the interview is a waste of your time, you've already sent out signals that you're more interested in yourself than the job.

- Respond to the **ground rules** carefully. Don't keep throwing in amusing anecdotes when the interviewer wants to get down to business.

- Avoid **name dropping** of individuals (it makes you sound like you have superior connections) but do mention the names of organisations you have worked for or with.

- Don't misjudge **casualness**. You may be the preferred

candidate, but being late, under-prepared or dressing down for the interview can undo much good work.

- Be **generous** – don't hold the floor, even though you have a million achievement stories at your fingertips. It's not your party, you're just the guest.

- **Start on a high**. Experienced introverts can be cautious or reserved. Prepare yourself to speak with enthusiasm from the outset, if necessary by telephoning a friend to explain energetically why you want the job five minutes before the interview starts.

- Don't **trash** yourself or anyone else. Experience sometimes comes hand in hand with cynicism. Irony plays badly in an interview, as does criticism of former employers.

- Exercise the **edit** button in advance and always think 'leave them wanting more'. Contain yourself. Nervous chatter also suggests you are covering something up. Experienced candidates tend to say far too much and in the process lose focus *and* give away negative information. Trim down epic stories into mini-narratives otherwise you cut the number of questions you will be asked. Give brief facts, not your life story, but include sufficient details to gain impact (see Chapter 13).

- Prepare to **hurdle** – plan ways you will get over the predictable barriers and problem questions, ranging from 'Why are you on the market?' to 'You don't have a degree …'. See Chapter 15 on predictable probing questions.

- Get **nervous**. If you have no anxiety at all about the conversation, you are either complacent or unexcited. Even if you are an experienced candidate, tomorrow's interview should involve adrenaline if it's worth doing. As Tiger Woods said: 'If you don't feel nervous, that means you don't care about how you play.'

- Don't be **over-confident**. Maybe it's worth glancing over the Category 1 list above?

CHAPTER ELEVEN

What will they ask me?

THIS CHAPTER LOOKS AT:

- Your best strategy for anticipating questions
- Getting into the interviewer's mindset
- Predicting the key items on the employer shopping list
- Emphasising organisational fit, attitude and working style

Every time I sit with a client and try to predict interview questions, it becomes clearer that there is little new under the sun. While in theory an interviewer could ask you anything at all, a large proportion of interview questions are entirely predictable. So why do we worry so much about what will come up, or the prospect of 'awkward' or 'difficult' questions? It could be nervous avoidance, but could also be an admission that we haven't really put enough effort into preparation. You might feel there are thousands of possible questions (a great excuse for not preparing for any of them), ignoring the fact that there are clearly some questions more likely and more important. The difference between success and failure may in fact rest on just a few questions.

SEEING THE MAIN AGENDA

One of the most frequent reasons candidates get lost in the interview process is that they haven't grasped the basics – the questions that are most likely to come up in *any* interview:

Twenty of the most frequent interview questions (and what's really under discussion)

QUESTION	THE REAL AGENDA BEHIND THE QUESTION
1. Tell us about yourself.	Help us out – give us a quick overview of the shape of your career or your key skills.
2. Why are you on the market?	Is there a problem with your past work performance? Are you moving on from choice or circumstances?
3. What did you like and dislike about your last job?	What motivates you, what switches you off, and how critical are you of your last employer?
4. How quickly do you pick things up?	Are you trainable? A fast learner?
5. How do you respond to supervision?	Do you respond well to instructions and feedback?
6. What is your impact on others?	What would your work colleagues say about your working style?
7. What do you add to teams?	How conscious are you of your natural team contribution?
8. Who was your best boss and who was the worst?	Who have you learned from? How difficult can you be as an employee?
9. What are you most proud of in your working life?	What have you achieved? What do you get excited about in work?

	QUESTION	THE REAL AGENDA BEHIND THE QUESTION
10.	What have been your greatest challenges?	Where have you been stretched beyond your comfort zone?
11.	What are your strengths and weaknesses?	Where are you most likely to excel – or more likely to be a problem?
12.	How flexible are you?	Are you going to stick rigidly to your job description?
13.	How have you added value to past roles?	Where have you gone beyond the requirements of the job?
14.	How do you respond to stress and pressure?	What will you actually be like in a busy workplace?
15.	Why should we choose *you* from a field of strong applicants?	What gives you an edge? How are we going to remember you when you've left the interview?
16.	What do you get excited or passionate about?	How much does work matter to you? How can we motivate you?
17.	What makes you angry?	Are you likely to upset colleagues through inappropriate behaviour?
18.	What changes do you expect to bring to this job?	How will you make a difference in the first few months of the job?
19.	What are your career goals?	Have you enjoyed one career with clear themes running through it, or a random series of jobs?
20.	Why do you want *this* job?	What makes this job the right next step for you in a coherent career story?

INSIDE THE MIND OF THE INTERVIEWER

To predict the questions most likely to come up you need to get into the mind of the interviewer. Interviewers have two big problems: there are always more questions than time, and it's unclear which questions will be effective. And they have one objective: to get the right result, which means retrieval of evidence credible enough to tick the items on the employer checklist. Some of that list is visible to you and some of it you have to intelligently guess at, but a checklist definitely exists. So instead of worrying about what *might* come up, focus hard on what probably *will* come up.

Some questions will inevitably arise from the claims made in your CV or application form, cover letter, and possibly also in competency statements (see Chapter 15 for more on competency-based interviews). These questions are entirely predictable, but be prepared for your evidence to be put under the microscope, particularly those areas which suggest you may not be perfect for the job.

Recruitment consultant Pauline Godley writes 'Some interviewers focus on finding reasons to decline people so the short list is strong, as opposed to getting the best from candidates. A cynical view, I know, but having received feedback on hundreds of interviews over the years there does seem to be a slant on the negative. There are some very astute, commercially focused employers who really do look for the best in candidates, but they are few and far between.'

From this it's clear that there may well be a focus on those relatively small number of areas where you don't match the job and therefore can be discounted. An important strategy for all of the topic areas listed below is to ask yourself 'What parts of my CV is the interviewer worrying or doubtful about?'

ATTITUDE

Your attitude is not just probed in questions, but revealed in everything you do – responding to instructions, the clothes you choose for the interview, the working style revealed by your stories. Naturally you wouldn't be reading this book if you weren't committed to showing real interest in the job – or would you? Employers repeatedly complain that candidates convey apathy rather than enthusiasm – they want *a* job, not necessarily *this* job.

It's best not to make direct statements about your attitude; for example, saying you are a 'self-starter' or 'a winner'. This might work on *The Apprentice*, but interviewers in fact feel more secure if they discover personal traits for themselves. Saying 'I am passionate about detail' may prompt an inexperienced interviewer to nod approvingly and make a note. You have only made a claim, not proved it – even if the interviewer approves, he or she has nothing to remember, which means that your evidence hasn't been absorbed. To another interviewer this kind of statement is so free of content it sounds like unconvincing boasting, and an invitation to begin aggressive probing.

Show them, don't tell them. Telling a story where you clearly gave attention to important details works much better and sticks in the interviewer's memory. Most new graduates this year are telling employers that they are highly motivated, self-starters, team players and will go the extra mile. Don't waste your breath making empty claims – let your attitude come out in memorable narratives, so that the interviewer comes to a conclusion without the point being over-signalled.

'FIT'

Organisational fit may seem like a matter of chemistry, which some people believe you have no control over (see Chapter 17 on personality issues), but in fact you do have a great deal of control over what you communicate, beginning with the first impression you create, and working through examples you provide of working with others. Judgements around organisational fit are made very quickly, largely in terms of behaviours that you can think about in advance:

- Be courteous and friendly to everyone you meet on the day.

- Don't dominate the conversation, as this is taken as a clear indication of how you will operate in a team situation. Listen to questions carefully without interrupting.

- Tune in to the flow of the interview so you get a sense of when it is appropriate for you to stop talking.

- Be flexible around the requirements of the interview day, particularly if they are changed at the last minute.

- Give appropriate evidence of co-operative and consultative working (matched, if necessary, by times where the buck stopped with you).

WORKING STYLE

An employer wants not only to know what you can do, but what the impact of your work is on others. Yes, you can manage a budget, but how many toes do you tread on in order to get at the information you need? How do you lead others, or respond to authority? If you need to cut costs, can you do so without causing a staff walkout? Bearing in mind that the main reason people leave a job is their relationship with their line manager, employers know that working relationships matter.

Think very hard about this issue if the person who is interviewing you is someone who you will have to work alongside. What is it about you that might be worrying them – perhaps you're too assertive, too bright, or they think you will be telling them how to do their job?

UNDERPINNING KNOWLEDGE

Knowledge is something that interviewers feel is rather easier to get at, largely because a great deal of it is certificated in qualifications or training. Nevertheless, you should think of each of these simply as headings. There are tens of thousands of courses and qualifications out there, yet candidates generally assume that interviewers know about all of them. Explain the things that excited you as part of your learning. What can you do now that you couldn't do before?

Learn to talk about training which was informal and not certificated, perhaps because you learned on the job. Be clear about specialist knowledge – think of times when colleagues asked your advice or sought you out as an expert.

CONSTRAINTS

Constraints are sometimes simple issues like the earliest date you can start. Other issues are more complex, and these matter if the decision maker sees them as potential deal-breakers, for example the question of a long commute to work or the need for relocation.

Pay levels can be a constraint, too, particularly if the employer feels you can be hired for a low salary (focus on what you will deliver, not what you will cost) or you are too expensive (show how you will be good value). Wherever possible talk about salary and other terms and conditions once you have been offered the job.

Do address constraints head-on if you believe they might be worrying the decision maker. So, for example, if you are half way through a part-time degree and this hasn't come up, find the chance to talk about how you are good at juggling study and work commitments. If issues like this are never discussed they can end up as reasons to turn you down.

SKILL RANGE AND LEVEL

With constraints resolved in the interviewer's mind, you can now roll your sleeves up and get through your skills. Remember to combine claims with evidence – identify your skills and provide evidence of where you have used them.

A professional interview will establish the skills you are comfortable using and your skill level. A weak interview might accept your answer 'I'm pretty good at using Excel', but this kind of answer does you no favours – terms like 'beginner', 'proficient' or 'pretty good' provide no meaningful data about ability and just lead to interviewer uncertainty.

Give examples at the top end of your skill range – times when you have done something difficult. Potential is attractive, but experience carries more weight: where exactly have you used this skill? What problems did you overcome? What were the actual results you achieved? How much support or supervision did you need?

Don't underestimate your skills, as people often do. Learn to talk enthusiastically about the skills you are good at and find satisfying to use (see the section on 'motivated skills' at the end of this chapter for a tool that will help you identify them). Talking about the skills you use outside work often gives a more rounded picture.

MOTIVATION

A related area is around the things that drive you. You may be asked directly about the things in your job you find give you the biggest 'buzz'. Think in advance about what these are – when you visualise work on a Sunday night, what activities and situations do you actively look forward to? Often these are around people, challenge, learning or solving problems, but everyone is different, and our motivators change as we grow older. Think about what works for you, and then match them to the role on offer; there's no point saying that you're motivated by innovation and change if the job involves neither.

LEARNING CURVE

When an interviewer is thinking about motivation, often the real question is about your learning curve. Every job is a learning curve, and the first part of that curve is about novelty and excitement.

How trainable are you, and how long will it take you to learn a new role and new ways of working? If there are skills you don't currently have, how quickly are you going to absorb them? Here it's usually enough to tell good stories about where you have been thrown in the deep end in the past and done well.

What happens when the curve levels out for you – what keeps you motivated in the long term? Good questions will focus on how you respond to the routine aspects of the job, and how long you are likely to stay in the same role. But if you don't get asked questions that allow you to give a full picture of your abilities here, then work it into another answer when you get the chance.

ACHIEVEMENTS

Your motivation is often revealed in your achievements, which are the best way of convincing an employer that you have done, and can do, the things you claim. Your CV should be full of them (make them measurable, interesting and punchy) but always have a few extra achievement stories up your sleeve ready for a probing interview.

Remember that achievement stories really are 'stories' – there should be an engagement factor (see Chapter 13). If your stories are remembered, your abilities are, too.

KILLER QUESTIONS

Yes, there may be some oddball questions or really tough ones. Again, the tougher ones can be predicted. You may well be asked where you want to be in five years' time – your answer will reflect how clear you are about your career story. You will almost certainly be asked about weaknesses as well as strengths. Don't allow yourself to be put on the spot by something you can see coming a mile off (but see Chapter 17 on oddball questions).

YOUR DISTINGUISHING FACTOR

If your skills, knowledge and attitude fit, an interviewer may still be looking for something else. The last question is often unstated, but it is essentially 'as we have a number of candidates who can do the job, why should we choose *you*?'

Prepare for that one – what is the special mix that makes you different? Maybe it will be simply that you have more enthusiasm, more interest, better questions, better evidence. What an employer is often thinking is 'How will I remember you after you have left this room?', and the answer is not just about information, but a combination of the same four factors that get salespeople remembered:

1   immediate positive impact;

2   matching your solution to the employer's problem;

3   offering credible responses to probing questions;

4   finding common ground and shared experiences (personal 'hooks' like this are very powerful).

Behind every inspired performance is the hard work of good preparation, readying you for the big questions to come.

MOTIVATED SKILLS

It's virtually impossible to get a picture of all your skills on your own. However, I have developed a tool, the **JLA Skill Cards,** to identify your top 10 motivated skills, i.e. the things you are good at and enjoy performing. A full range of exercises are provided, enabling you to communicate your skills in terms of career highlights and achievements. The cards come with a full set of instructions plus exercises to help you identify skill gaps, your learning agenda, and ways of communicating your skills through achievement stories.

See **www.johnleescareers.com/skillsCards.asp** for details.

CHAPTER TWELVE

Pitching your message

WHAT MESSAGE?

A century ago when we were much more tolerant of the spoken word, you might have listened to a speech lasting two hours and then gone home able to repeat much of the content. In an age of information overload we absorb and transfer relatively simple bursts of information – sound-bites and bullet points. Asked why we choose one brand or another in a purchasing decision, the answer is normally a very brief bundle of facts, emotional responses and instinct – things just appeal to us, or look good value.

Decisions like this generally hang on three or four 'reasons' – a term to use carefully, because often such choices are far from logical. The same is true when people get recommended or in a hiring decision. You will have hundreds of pieces of information in your CV and may communicate 20–30 good points in an interview, but even with detailed note-taking an interviewer is only going to remember half of what you said, and will act upon a small handful of pieces of evidence. How do we know? Ask an interviewer what impressed her about a candidate, and you get three to four items. Ask why someone got the job, the number of reasons is about the same. We deal in shorthand. Make that fact work in your favour by deciding what messages you are going to leave in the mind of the interviewer.

BEING MEMORABLE

Simple messages matter because interviewers retain only a small amount of information about candidates. They take interview notes and may cover a lot of territory, but only a small amount of what you say will be noticed, and even less remembered. What will someone remember about you? You could of course leave that to chance. You might assume that your main skills or achievements will be remembered. Don't be too sure about that.

One way or another, interviewers work to a checklist, and once you have provided evidence of an area of competency the interviewer will probably make a note and move on. The kinds of things that do stick in their memory are those that make you stand out in a good or bad way. If you don't address these in advance you may either miss an opportunity to shine, or deliver a negative message without meaning to. These things can be entirely random – something you do or say during the interview or even the way you look.

Being memorable is essential if you hope to get through to second interview or get a job offer. So you need to decide in advance what impression you want to make, and what you want the interviewer to remember, making sure that if only three or four things are remembered these are all *reasons why you fit the job*.

Taking control of your message is about *making sure that the interviewer gets to hear the things you want to talk about.* Focus on the three to four elements you believe really matter to the employer, and then provide one or two additional items of information about why you are different from a run-of-the mill candidate. To some this sounds like devilish manipulation, but it really isn't – it's simply making sure you get through *your* agenda for a meeting and present yourself as the best candidate for the job.

It's important to always keep in mind that this doesn't mean 'How many different things can I say about myself?' Instead think about the things which are most important to the employer and how you can deliver them. This may be even more important if your interviewer is not highly skilled.

Careers specialist Loraine Bones writes: 'Not all interviewers have been professionally trained in recruitment practices (they may be professional accountants, engineers, systems analysts or whatever). As such, you may feel that you haven't been given the right opportunities to present your case. Under these circumstances it is vital to take the initiative and "engineer" an opening in the discussion to present your evidence of suita-bility. Never leave the interview feeling you have sold yourself short!'

Whatever your messages, make sure you communicate them. Some highly skilled candidates fail to get beyond the first interview stage simply because they sit back and wait for the right questions to come along, or fail to mention things because they are already in the CV.

NEGATIVE INFORMATION STICKS

Interviewers 'tune out' for some part of the interview. Our brains are perfectly capable of listening to interview answers *and* thinking about the traffic, tonight's match, or what to buy for supper. Conducting an interview is not always an inspiring process, so the interviewer is quite likely to be thinking about other things during the conversation, just as you are not always fully attentive when undertaking a routine task like driving a car or mowing the lawn. Interviewers frequently tune out by starting to think about their next question rather than listening to your answer. At other times they are thinking about something you said earlier, not really listening to your carefully prepared evidence, particularly if it all sounds rather dull and predictable.

What always gets an interviewer's attention is where you say something negative about yourself or somewhere you worked. It might be a throw-away line joking about your lack of wisdom. It might be a comment about a former boss or employer. Either way, you can guarantee that the interviewer's attention jumps back, and if you've got their attention, you've planted something in memory.

But was it something you wanted the interviewer to remember? This is the big danger of unplanned over-delivery – if you ramble on, sooner or later you will say something negative. Focusing on your message means you need to think first of all about the topics you don't want to be remembered for.

'LIFEBOAT ANSWERS'

You should never go near an interview without some short, pre-packaged responses around the most vulnerable topics. These are short, upbeat statements which get you past a negative point and move you onto positive ground. What topics should they cover? Anything that will throw you off your game in the interview. This could be about gaps in your CV, strengths and weaknesses, reasons for leaving past jobs, how up to date your learning is, or your job search history. These questions leave you feeling all at sea. They are entirely predictable, and so is their effect if you are unprepared for them – you are going to squirm and shuffle. So take them seriously, and prepare for choppy waters.

Your aim here is to have a series of short, ready-made statements that keep the interviewer happy, make a strong point in your favour, and allow the conversation to move on quickly. You cannot achieve that aim by thinking on your feet in the interview room itself. That strategy will lead to you floundering and splashing about and losing all sense of what is actually happening in the interview.

Instead, you need to stock your lifeboat with safety equipment in advance – your pre-prepared 'lifeboat answers' (an idea which builds on the Presentation Statements concept developed by careers specialist Bernard Pearce).

Talk through dangerous question areas with a friend. For example, if you worry about being asked 'Why were you made redundant from your last job?' rehearse an answer that shows the experience was not about you ('like a lot of people I was offered terms when the organisation restructured') and shift the focus to the future ('it's been a good opportunity to rethink what I want to get out of my career, and has shown me that this is the kind of role I would really like').

Start by sketching out your answers as bullet points on paper, try them out loud, and then try them on someone who knows what will and won't fly in a real interview situation. Don't learn them word for word because they won't sound like they match the question, but take even more care here to control your material, and be brief. Get a trusted friend to ask you the questions you don't want to be asked, and practise your 'lifeboat answers' at least three times. That way they will be secure, tested, and ready to rescue you from the stormy deep.

YOUR QUESTIONS ARE PART OF YOUR MESSAGE

Decision makers frequently comment on the fact that strong candidates put in a performance that is sustained right until

the end, which includes some good quality questions. Sital
Ruparelia, Host of Career Management TV, says 'the questions
a candidate asks tell me much more about their thought process
and intellect than the prepared answers they provide'. For the
interviewer this moment will probably be the easiest part to
remember, so plan in advance to ask questions which confirm
your overall message. For example, if you want to show you
have a lively, enquiring mind, don't ask questions like 'What
exactly do you do here?'

Go beyond the surface level ('How does this job fit in?') and
don't waste time asking questions which are more appropriate
after a job offer has been made ('Is there a pension scheme?').
You could ask for more details about initiatives you have seen
mentioned in the press, or questions which show your curiosity
about new product lines, but these are better for small talk at
the beginning.

The best questions are about *your future in the job* (for
example, ask about how the job will change, what opportunities you will have for personal development or working with
other teams). This reinforces a picture of you in the job, the
same picture you have been building throughout.

SO WHAT?

When you try to get your key messages across you'll be
wondering how they are being received. If you're getting lots of
nodding and other positive signals, great – these are all buying
signals. If you are not getting much back it could be for a variety
of reasons. You might need more practice. You might be offering
messages which are not as effective or as matched to the role as
you imagine. You could feel that the interviewer is thinking 'so
what?' If so, remember there are three kinds of 'so what?':

1   **So what?** You're telling me something I hear all the time –
    I can't differentiate you from other candidates.

2   **So what?** I get it, but you haven't yet sold the idea to me in language I can get excited about.

3   **So what?** I like what I hear and I am interested, but I genuinely need your help to work out how we can match your 'offer' to our needs.

You know what kind of 'so what?' you're getting from the level of interest. If the interviewer isn't really listening it's probable that you've failed to get past first base. If you're getting cautious encouragement you may be getting a category 2 response, but if you are getting detailed questions and requests for clarification you are probably hitting level 3. You've got someone to remember the kind of message that gives you a real edge. Be absolutely clear about how your 'offer' matches to their needs – don't leave this to chance or the employer's skill at interpretation.

HOW WILL YOUR MESSAGE TRAVEL WITHOUT YOU?

You'll already have recognised that some jobs aren't advertised and the only way you come across them is through actively networking your way into conversations with employers. There is only one real measure of success here: *how often your name comes up in your absence.*

An invitation to talk about an unadvertised job is a gift. You're in a short list of one, and you have more influence over job content, salary and other negotiable points. So how does your name come up as a potential candidate? It's still all about messages. Making sure that your name comes up is about being visible, talking to people, following your curiosity, finding out about organisations and sectors.

Just as you hope to plant three punchy pieces of evidence in an interview, you can do the same thing when networking. If asked 'What are you looking for?', your answer should not be a job title, but those key messages you want someone to pass on.

If your name crops up as a recommendation it's rare that more than a handful of reasons will be mentioned. I often ask clients to put their CVs away and just talk to me for 90 seconds about what they would like someone to say when recommending them. They usually start with words like 'reliable', 'well-motivated', or 'creative'. Those are the adjectives used by this year's graduates; unless you want to send out the same undifferentiated message as everyone else, think again. The most transportable messages seem to fall into the following categories:

Role summary – How would you like to be labelled? This might not be your last job title but something more descriptive, e.g. 'change management specialist in the finance sector'.

Primary skill set – What are you known for? What do you excel at?

Know-how – What areas of work do you know about? What is your specialist knowledge?

Personal hooks – People often remember shared or memorable connections, interests or hobbies.

Personality – the above information may be topped off with something extra about how easy you are to work with or your impact on others.

CHAPTER THIRTEEN

Getting your story across

WHY STORIES WORK

'Tell stories instead of giving scripted answers,' writes career coach Sital Ruparelia, 'authentic stories tailored to individual roles and employers.'

You might feel uncomfortable with the idea of stories, either because you're not a natural raconteur or because stories seem a long way from the hard world of business and facts. Think again. We're *not* talking about 'telling stories' in the sense of telling lies. Well-rounded examples command attention, and wake up even the most jaded interviewer. The 'story' aspect to interviews has two important dimensions:

1 Short mini-narratives work because they engage, entertain, and like all stories are memorable. We like stories and remember them better than bald facts. We like good yarns and pass them on to other people.

2   Interviewers are generally more comfortable if the job on offer fits into your overall 'career story'.

Stories are not just memorable, but draw you into another world for a few moments. When you're drawn in you start to 'picture the scene' – in other words, really visualise someone else's experience. This helps in the subtle art of impression management where you are working hard to get an interviewer to picture you doing the job.

Narratives also form bonds between speaker and listener – while enjoying the story you really see the perspective of the person telling it. Once you inhabit someone else's point of view, it's hard not to align yourself in other ways too, seeing how much you have in common.

FINDING SAFETY IN STORYLINES

Narratives are easier to remember than facts, so allow you to move smoothly and quickly into answer mode. Imagine you're asked the question 'How do you manage difficult customers?' What happens next? Your brain isn't like a hard drive, flicking instantly to a data file. You're rapidly thinking: 'What can I remember? Is it relevant, interesting? Will it survive a round of probing questions?' On the surface you may maintain swan-like elegance, but below the water you are paddling fast. By the time a reasonable answer emerges, what has happened? You've lost focus on the all-important task of maintaining rapport with the interviewer.

Know where the story is going before you open your mouth. This does not mean having every sentence pre-recorded in memory – that makes you sound like an answering machine. However, it helps to have key phrases ready, particularly for beginnings, endings, and where you talk about achievements. If you know you are going to be asked about dealing with under-motivated colleagues, it's no good planning in a general way ('I guess I'll say something about my coaching experience') – plan for the actual words you will use ('I've had the opportunity to coach several members of my team who were demotivated and under-performing. My approach was ...').

Narrative-rich evidence helps people remember you, but only if the stories feel like they're yours. Edinburgh-based career coach Margaret Middlemiss writes: 'I find that people go to interviews and leave their personality behind, trying very hard to remember the "buzz words" and talk in a language they think the company wants to hear or say what the textbook says. This doesn't come across as genuine.'

MATCH STORIES CAREFULLY

Learn how to stress different parts of the story in response to different questions. Build a story around key areas. Like any good communicator, tailor your material to the needs of your audience – be firmly in control of your 'edit', 'pause' and 'stop' buttons in the interview room.

While the biggest danger in interviews is lack of preparation, there are dangers with stories that are *too* polished. Accomplished narrators can sometimes entertain themselves too much and not know when to stop. Jane Downes, author of *The Career Book*, writes of the dangers of 'being over-scripted and over-reliant on a certain suite of questions coming your way. Give the interviewers a whiff that you're trying to prompt their questions in a pre-ordained direction, and you've succeeded in alienating them. Show discomfort when they throw you a curve ball, and you've lost serious credibility.'

HR consultant Karen Kinnear says: 'The big issue with candidates who have not been interviewed for some time and who have just read up on competency-based interviews is they sometimes group their interview "stories" under competency headings. For example, they will have a couple of "stories" prepared that they feel demonstrate strong leadership skills and use them whether or not the examples fit the question being asked. Be aware that your stories provide evidence of a range of competencies, so it is important to listen carefully to the question being asked and choose the most relevant story.'

LEARN THE NARRATOR'S ART

- **The voice matters**. You wouldn't entertain friends with a story told in a monotone, matter-of-fact manner. A good storyteller uses a tone of voice that is really saying 'listen carefully, because I am going to tell you something very interesting'. Rehearse good opening and linking phrases, and even the odd cliff-hanger (e.g. 'what happened next knocked me for six').

- **Tell the story from the inside**. A tale is told from a particular point of view, either by someone who was present when events happened, or by a narrator. Clearly in an interview you need to sound like someone right at the centre of events.

- **An arresting opening** grabs the attention. Think about the opening words you use to tell a story related to a skill. There's a big difference between 'I used communication skills when ...' and 'Let me tell you about a time I was thrown in the deep end'.

- **Jump straight into the story**. In interviews most candidates spend too long setting the scene. Tell the story of the problem, certainly ('We had to make a big impact quickly with no budget'), but don't bore the listener with excessive background information ('My department is part of a larger division with a matrix management structure ...'). Focus on what you hope will be remembered.

- **Make your material come alive**. Use the present tense sometimes ('so I'm in the control room and all the red lights have come on at the same time ...').

- **Move from familiarity into strangeness.** Begin with shared ground, and then take the listener into new territory (for example, describe a familiar scenario such as a difficult customer, but then show how you tried a fresh approach).

- **Invite the listener in.** The big idea behind storytelling isn't information, but sharing, inviting people in. We tell people stories because we want to make them welcome and feel included through a sense of openness, and the story should do that for you. Try using phrases like 'I don't know if you've ever been in this situation, but ...'

- **A telling phrase** helps to pinpoint what you are trying to say. Avoid clichés such as 'bottom line' or 'turned the business around', but find words that capture what was going on in fresh language that brings events to life.

- **Draw a picture.** Rather than saying 'We had a meeting', say 'It was 6.30pm and there were seven of us crammed in a small office throwing in suggestions – it was wild, but it worked.'

- **Don't try to be more important than the story.** As candidates start to become confident they begin to embellish stories and throw in asides. If the details are not part of the story, keep them out. Don't tell more stories than the interviewer needs to hear, and don't hog the stage for too long.

- **Every audience is different.** Stories don't work all the time, and every listener is different. Some people will clearly be drawn in and engaged, others will be more distant. Also, don't judge your impact on lack of feedback – the interviewer may still remember every word.

ROSE-TINTED ANSWERS

As Chapter 16 on probing questions outlines, too many candidates show every event through rose-tinted glasses. Have a few examples up your sleeve of times things went wrong; for example, a time you worked in a dysfunctional team or with a difficult customer.

The reason these answers work better is obvious in story terms. Stories work well where there is drama, conflict and opposition. Narratives that don't include this and move simply from problem to solution quickly bore us. Since we find a diet of happy endings unconvincing and dull, vary your approach. Talk about times when things were difficult or didn't have a great conclusion. Make sure you rehearse these tales, because a rough-cut, improvised answer could simply semaphore a message of incompetence.

However, a story which shows you adapting to circumstances and making the most of a difficult situation will always sound more convincing and will be more memorable; they also show important qualities including a sense of perspective, the ability to learn from experience, and an understanding that you can't win in every situation.

Career coach Kate Howlett has developed an exciting model around storytelling and I am delighted to reprint it below. If at first it seems slightly fanciful, remember that this approach has achieved great results with the most hard-nosed clients.

Where are the sequins?

What formula has worked for hundreds of years? The only one that has stood the test of time is the fairy story. Fairy stories were spoken aloud and passed on from one generation to the next. Think about how they begin: 'Once upon a time, in a far off land, there was a handsome prince.' Build the story properly – too many people just jump straight in with their achievements and wonder why the interviewer isn't impressed. Build the context up properly – what was the situation, the problem?

This is of course closely related to the workplace. 'Once upon a time in a far off land' translates into 'Three years ago when I was working at ABC as their finance director ...'. Next, introduce the characters, the wicked witch, the big bad wolf, and of course the hero – you. You need to be at the centre of the story so that it's not the story of the project or the team, but the story of what you did. Keep the hero at the centre of the story.

Build the adventure, because every fairy story is an adventure: rivers to cross, mountains to climb, dragons to slay. It's OK if things went wrong, because that shows learning and the ability to recover from disaster. Build the tension, too. Describe how as the hero you pitted your wits, won over, came up trumps. A good fairy story ends 'happily ever after'. How did your story end? What were the long-term effects of your actions in the organisations you worked in?

Building the story means focusing on memorable details. Think of the way the princess in a fairy story is described – her golden tresses, the fabric of her dress. These are story details that stay with us, so sometimes you need to describe the sequins. When someone finishes the interview, what three or four sequins will they remember? Look at your story and ask yourself 'Where is the hero? Where is the dragon? Where are the sequins?'

Learn to tell the story out loud. Fairy stories were designed to be heard, so it's vital you speak the stories. Start by writing down the key details, then speak the story out loud. The first time you do so will score about 3 out of 10. Practise it twice again; it's amazing, but by the time you tell the story for the third time you will be closer to 9 out of 10. Get feedback if you can, but trust

▶

in the fact that you will hear most problems yourself. Have plenty of stories ready. Imagine them in coloured boxes in the interview room with you, ready to be opened.

Kate Howlett, Ruspini Consulting

CHAPTER FOURTEEN

It's not a standard interview – how do I play it?

SECOND INTERVIEWS

A rule of thumb among careers specialists is that a first interview confirms that you can do the job, while a second interview checks whether you will fit in. There's a lot of truth in that. Sometimes the first interview is with HR to establish if you have the right skill set, and the second interview is with a line manager, so questions will be much more job specific. A second interview is sometimes simply a chance for other staff members to check you out, or can be a final stamp of approval from a senior member of staff. Find out as much as you can about the reason for each stage; ask who will be interviewing you, and what areas you should prepare for.

Sometimes a second interview will explicitly pick up on your answers from the first round, probing areas which still provide concerns. Concentrate on those parts of your first interview where you gave answers which did not fully address the question. Think of different and better examples – you should raise your game at a second interview rather than putting in the same performance. However, don't assume that a second interview will follow logically from the first. Interview notes may have been passed on, but if the same questions come up, answer them as thoroughly as before.

PANEL INTERVIEWS

Panel interviews are widely used, particularly for public sector or charity appointments. The idea behind panel interviews is that objectivity is improved by using multiple interviewers, but there is in fact little evidence that panel interviews are more accurate than one-to-one versions. Panels can be swayed by all kinds of agendas, or dominated by the most senior person present. Furthermore, panels often feel far more constrained than individual interviewers to work to a script, leaving far less opportunity to probe candidates' answers.

A panel interview may not be something you look forward to. It can feel more intimidating, and it feels harder to build rapport with several people at once. Who do you look at when you answer a question? Panel interviews have more formality about them with less opportunity for small talk, so often candidates respond in kind by acting in a much stiffer, more artificial way.

As with any interview, find out who is on the panel, their background, and what they want to hear. One member of the panel may come to find you and take you into the room – that's an important opportunity to talk about the organisation if you have time. When you are in the room, note the names of panel members as they are introduced. That way you can respond to questions by occasionally using someone's name.

Work out who the main decision maker is (this may be clear from the paperwork or from the website, but if in doubt ask in advance) and give that person due attention, but communicate with everyone. Sometimes there are people present who will ask few or no questions, but don't ignore them – make eye contact with a number of people during each answer.

Remember that panel interviews are constraining for interviewers because they have less opportunity to really get to know you. Also, panels usually contain a few people who rarely conduct interviews, so you may have to work co-operatively to make sure that their awkward questions prompt the right answer. Panels give interviewers much more power, and sometimes interviewers ask sticky questions without giving you a chance to warm up. If so, take a moment to compose your thoughts – well-structured answers matter here more than anywhere else.

If a panel probes your answers, roll with the punches. If your answers aren't probed at all, it may be that the panel is limited to set questions, so you need to work differently because your first answer may be taken as final. If so, add detail to your answers and make sure you address all parts of the competencies required. You might ask directly 'Does that cover what you need, or would it be helpful if I provided some more detail?' You might even probe yourself – 'I expect you'd like to know a little bit more about how I sold that budget cut ...'

Remember that panel members will usually have at least a few moments between each interview to compare thoughts, so concentrate on a strong opening and a positive ending. The final stage of the interview will be strongest in memory, so it matters that you ask one or two good questions at the end, and look confident as you say goodbye to each member by name, shaking each person's hand and thanking them for their time.

TELEPHONE SCREENING INTERVIEWS

Employers increasingly use telephone interviews for a quick screening process, checking candidates against a brief set of criteria. In this situation prepare your evidence and wait for the questions. Don't be disappointed if the interviewer seems to take little interest and doesn't want to get a bigger picture – the function of this kind of interview is to screen you in or out, so there's little point trying to throw in extra information.

More detailed telephone interviews require the same preparation as face-to-face exchanges, with some important exceptions. You will not be visible (unless it's a video interview – see below), so you cannot communicate anything by your appearance, gestures or body language. Your voice has to do all the work, including establishing a relationship. Use your voice actively – think about volume, pace and pitch so that you *sound* interested and enthusiastic – try smiling when you talk. If you need a bit of extra confidence, take the phone call standing up. Answer clearly, which might mean *slightly* more slowly than normal, and briefly – it's even easier for the interviewer to switch off. At the end ask if there is anything else you can add, and ask your own questions too.

Other useful tips are:

1   Find a quiet room to take the call without *any* interruptions or background noise (never try to undertake an interview from a train or in a public place).

2   Have in front of you the same information you would take into an interview.

3   When you answer the phone, announce your name with enthusiasm, and don't start sounding flat, or as if you've been interrupted.

4   Make notes as you talk to keep you focused.

5   Accept any invitation for small talk at the beginning and

the end of the interview as this is your only chance to build a relationship.

6   Be sure you know the name of the person interviewing you and use that name from time to time.

Phone interviews seem informal, so job seekers sometimes take their eye off the ball. If you take the call at your desk, turn your computer OFF, otherwise you will be reading emails or consulting Google while you are speaking, as your voice will reveal. You do not have time during a telephone interview to look up documents to retrieve extra information – print important items in advance.

Have a Plan B for calls that come in at unexpected times. Keep a printed activity sheet to hand to remind you of the names of organisations and people you have approached. If the interviewer calls at an unscheduled time, gather your thoughts and take the interview if you possibly can, otherwise you might miss that day's schedule. If you really are not ready, arrange a time to call back when you have had a chance to prepare properly.

VIDEO INTERVIEWS

Twenty years ago it was predicted that by now all interviews would use video technology, but they are still relatively rare. However, web-based interviews are now growing in popularity as with the growth of Skype and similar packages. Be careful with Skype – make sure the camera on your computer is switched off unless you deliberately choose to let the interviewer see you on screen. You may be invited into a business centre or office to join in an interview using higher quality connection. Sometimes video interviews are recorded by external selectors, using questions set by the company. The advantage of this approach is that managers can see each candidate answering the same questions, and can compare responses. You can consider these very much like the kind of interview that will be conducted by recruitment consultants (see Chapter 3).

The rules for video interviews are an adaptation of what you need to do in telephone interviews. You are not in the room, so body language and gestures will not have the same effect and may even be difficult to interpret on screen. What you are wearing will be visible, so dress accordingly. Check out in advance how you appear on camera. If you have a webcam on your computer, record yourself giving some pre-rehearsed answers, and you'll see there is often a time lag between sound and picture, and audio is not always as clear as it could be. This is a good reason to make sure that you don't answer too quickly, and don't move about while talking. When you are interviewed, look at the camera rather than your screen, otherwise you will always appear to be looking down. Be aware if you use a webcam that the microphone usually picks up all the noise in the room, so don't shuffle papers.

ASSESSMENT CENTRES

Candidates often feel stressed by the prospect of an assessment centre. An assessment centre is an event where candidates are brought together to undertake a range of assessment activities. These can include intelligence, personality and other tests; group exercises including discussion, goal-setting and team activities; in-tray exercises; and you may also need to give a presentation. The assessment event will often include at least one interview, and feedback from specialist assessors including occupational psychologists.

Assessment centres are expensive and time-consuming, but are statistically more penetrating and effective than any single method used alone. Their focus is on predicting job performance and they should offer a thorough, in-depth assessment. For candidates they are demanding but often positive experiences, and sometimes include helpful feedback. Sometimes these events are competitive if there is one or more jobs to be won; at other times there is a fixed standard so no one, or everyone, may be selected.

If you are invited to one, look carefully at the joining instructions and then do not be afraid to ask for further information if anything else is unclear. An assessment centre is a complicated event, and very few people understand exactly what they have to do, and what standards they are supposed to reach, simply by reading the invitation letter.

Ask for full details of the various tests and events you will experience, and then use the Internet to research them – many providers offer online samples of tests and other materials such as in-tray and group exercises. Rely as much on your personal research as the information you are sent by the employer.

Interviews conducted during the day at assessment centres may be identical to the kind of detailed, probing questioning you might receive in any context. Often the interview will also probe aspects of your personality and working style that have come out at the event itself.

Give particular attention to group tasks or discussions as these are strong indicators of leadership potential, team interaction, communication skills and decision making. In discussions seek others' opinions and make suggestions, and don't try to dominate conversations; include everyone in the discussion, but be decisive if the task requires it.

Be aware of the most frequent reasons people do badly at assessment centres. One is poor preparation through inadequate attention to briefing materials, another is allowing your overall performance to be knocked back by difficulties experienced on one task. Others are routine interview flaws writ large – lack of research on the organisation or sector, superficial awareness of challenges being faced, a poor understanding of what is required in the role, and a failure to anticipate questions.

'INFORMAL' INTERVIEWS

It's always an interview, whether it's in the board room, Starbucks, or on the golf course. Even if you're assured that it is 'just a conversation', be prepared.

If you are invited to an interview over a meal, that effectively means you've got to the second interview stage – the employer knows you can do the job well but wants to get to know what kind of person you are. A relaxed setting can encourage you to drop your guard, but also presents a good opportunity to find out about the organisation and role.

If it really is an interview over a meal remember three things: don't choose an expensive item, don't choose a dish which you will end up wearing, and avoid alcohol. Don't forget that you may be being assessed on your social skills, especially if it is a role where you may be entertaining clients.

CHAPTER FIFTEEN

How do I shine at a competency-based interview?

THIS CHAPTER LOOKS AT:

- Covering more than the basics of competency-based interviews
- Why the process looks deceptively simple
- What goes wrong when you wing it
- Ways of standing out from the crowd

REVISITING THE ESSENTIALS

In the world of Human Resources there are two terms in play – 'competence' and 'competency'. The Chartered Institute of Personnel and Development (CIPD) outlines a technical difference: '"Competency" is now generally defined as the behaviours that employees must have, or must acquire, to input into a situation in order to achieve high levels of performance, while 'competence' relates to a system of minimal standards or is demonstrated by performance and outputs.' As Michael Armstrong wrote in his article 'Demystifying Competence', 'try telling that to a line manager'.

In the world of work the terms are used interchangeably. A competency is not just about what you do, but how you do it. From a candidate perspective you don't need to worry about the theory of competencies, but you do need to give attention to the way they are being used by recruiting organisations.

A good working definition of a *competency* is 'a combination of skills, knowledge and personal qualities which enables an employee to carry out specific tasks at an effective or superior level of performance'. You will notice that a competency is therefore not the same as a skill. A skill is purely about action. Van driving is a skill. A proficient van driver making local deliveries will also possess underlying knowledge (route planning), will have measurably good driving skills (measured by testing or a clean complaints record), and will probably have a flexible and relaxed manner with customers.

Competencies are therefore a mix of five elements:

1   **Skill** – the tasks completed (e.g. designing a PowerPoint presentation).

2   **Knowledge** – having an underpinning knowledge (what the software is capable of achieving, how to get the desired results from the options available).

3   **Behaviours** – what an observer can see (completing the presentation accurately and on time).

4   **Attitude** – the state of mind which underlies activity (using imagination, considering the needs of the end user, taking care and attending to detail).

5   **Impact** – how others experience, remember and feel about your contribution (doing a great job is noticed by the Marketing Director).

A NOTE ON IMPACT

To be strictly accurate, 'impact' doesn't appear in most competency statements, but is probably more important than anything else. We often make the mistake of believing our career performance is judged by an overview of everything we have done in a working year, summarised in an appraisal report.

However, all the evidence for why people get promoted or attached to interesting projects is that they are noticed in one or two peak moments with good outcomes. This might, for example, be when you are presenting information to senior staff, leading a project, researching something that really matters to the organisation. In these key moments someone important gets a quick but decisive glimpse of you doing something important, and doing it well. You have done things, consciously or not, which have made you visible to decision makers at critical moments.

These moments are often about emotional impact. The American poet Maya Angelou wrote: 'I've learned that people will forget what you said, people will forget what you did, but people will never forget how you made them feel.' Impressing someone, going the extra mile, really focusing on what your employer is most excited about – these are all characteristics that get you noticed and considered for future roles. You bring this into the interview by mentioning in passing how people showed their response to your actions, for example by sending a personal thank-you note or recommending you to others.

DIFFERENT WAYS YOU WILL ENCOUNTER COMPETENCIES

Competency-based interviews are common and very much part of the fabric of recruitment and selection. You may come across them in a variety of ways:

● A list of competencies is provided showing how each

will be measured. You will probably be asked to write
statements describing how you match each competency.

● Sometimes competencies are listed but it is not clear
   how they will be measured. In this case highlight your
   competencies in your documentation and at interview.

● A list of competencies is provided, but it is clear that other
   factors are also going to be considered. Broad preparation
   is required, as well as working out the employer's
   shopping list (see Chapter 7).

● You suspect that the employer has some competencies in
   mind, but they are not listed. Here you have to do even
   more homework reading between the lines and pulling in
   whatever information you can from people who know the
   organisation well.

● A discussion of competencies comes up informally during
   an interview. Having more than a few pre-prepared
   narratives is a vital line of defence.

HOW COMPETENCY-BASED INTERVIEWS LOOK DECEPTIVELY SIMPLE

Competency-based questions are a form of behavioural
interviewing – focusing closely on past events and life situations. According to the CIPD, about 6 out of 10 employers
currently use some kind of competency framework. Why do
competencies appeal to employers? They have some value in
increasing objectivity, and there is certainly evidence to suggest
that a structured interview looking at competencies is more
likely to give an accurate result than the rambling, 'friendly
chat' which passes for an interview in some organisations.
However, perhaps the real reason is that this approach uses
tick-boxes and matrices, which make the selection process *look*
fairer and more scientific. Used well (and sparingly), selection
of competencies requires employers to think about the skills

and qualities which provide above-average workplace performance, and encourages answers based on evidence rather than bragging.

The great mismatch in the marketplace is this. Employers are keen to examine competencies (but not always good at drawing them out of candidates). Candidates have little interest in competencies (they would much rather talk about more tangible things like skills, qualifications, attitude to work), and make the mistake of believing that talking about competencies is a stroll in the park.

Far from it. Your responsibility to deliver is even greater than in a standard interview – you've got to structure your answer, know where to begin and end, and make sure it hits the target, at the right standard, and in the right language. Don't get fogged by complicated language – the backbone of your approach needs to be narrative: 'Let me tell you about a time when ... the problem I was dealing with was. This was my approach ... this was the outcome.' For each competency you will be developing a good short story.

Simple enough. So why are these interviews 'deceptively simple'? Because there are hidden dimensions. First, you need to think carefully about language. You may have everything being sought, but if you don't describe your competencies in the language an employer understands, immediately, you're missing the target. Look carefully at the competency statements and look also at language used by the organisation on its website and in other documents. For example, you may have managed budgets in the past, but this employer is looking for cost control. Translating your experience into language which is immediately meaningful to an employer is vital if you are switching from one sector to another.

Second, think about depth and breadth, the invisible dimensions. How much detail you need to give depends very much on the culture and style of the organisation. Some interview situations will simply give you an opportunity to describe an example of where you demonstrated a particular ability. A short, snappy answer won't work if an interview panel does not allow itself supplementary questions, so in that context you need to offer a more developed answer. You need to practise setting the scene for your answer so you don't go straight for the punch line; however, do be aware that too much scene-setting causes an interviewer to switch off.

That's depth. Breadth is about the way you use answers to introduce other skills, qualities and areas of experience that are not necessarily part of the competency framework, but may make you the preferred candidate. For example, an answer on teamwork might show not just your ability to win over difficult colleagues but your verbal communication skills.

SIX (SLIGHTLY SUBVERSIVE) RULES FOR PREPARING FOR COMPETENCY-BASED INTERVIEWS

1   *Do* the preparation. It's a no-brainer. You have been told exactly what an employer is looking for, and you've been warned that against each competency someone is going to ask a question beginning 'Tell me about a time when you …' So prepare your evidence carefully and thoroughly. See Chapter 13 for tips on preparing mini-narratives.

2   **Prepare in depth.** Don't just prepare surface level stories: 'Sure, I can tell you about a time when I led a team. I recruited a great team at XYZ. I motivated everyone and we hit our targets.' Everything sounds good, but your evidence is as thin as a coat of gloss paint. How did you achieve this? What barriers did you overcome? What went wrong? What would you do differently next time? Think of each example as a problem you solved, and be prepared for probing questions.

3   **Prepare supplementary evidence.** You may already have provided evidence of competencies in an application form

or in your CV. What other examples can you come up with?

4   **Read between the lines.** You may be dealing with a long list of competencies. Research – through contacts, employer website research, talking to a recruiter – which ones matter most. What skills or knowledge isn't listed that might also be interesting to an employer? Sifting ahead of time, so you pitch the right information, marks you out as an above-average candidate.

5   **Don't leave gaps.** What if you don't have the competency? Think hard, because you are probably under-selling yourself. Offer strong, compensatory evidence which matches as closely as possible – for example, if you don't have a particular qualification, describe your skill and knowledge level in such a way that it is clear you know more than someone who has the qualification but insufficient experience.

6   **Throw in something different.** You have no idea how boring it is to conduct competency-based interviews listening to repetitive, dull evidence. Throw in something surprising – an unusual problem, an unusual solution to a problem, perhaps examples that are taken from outside the world of work. Competency frameworks encourage dull interviews. Be different.

STRUCTURING YOUR ANSWERS

Faced with a printed list of competencies, it's easy to think you can cover all the bases with detailed preparation. It's a good place to start, of course. You will be asked a question about each competency identified, and you will need to provide evidence from your experience that you can meet the required standard.

There are various models around to help you give a

structured answer to a competency-based question. Here is mine, first published in *Take Control of Your Career*:

The Skills Triangle

The three-part skills story works, essentially, because you are conveying the information that employers find useful and interesting. The three parts of your story in fact fit into the **Skills Triangle** shown below – a great way of remembering or recording skills.

FIGURE 15.1 *The Skills Triangle*

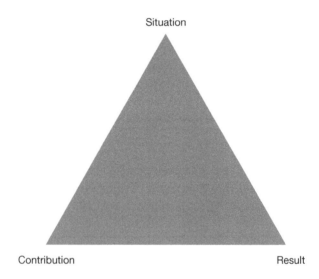

Situation: A time, place and context where you used a particular skill. It doesn't have to be an earth-shattering event. Even the small stuff picks up your skill set. Describe the size and nature of the problem you faced.

Contribution: Next, talk about what *you* did (rather than 'we', the team or the organisation). Talking about what you did should again contain enough detail to reveal the key ingredients of a competency – skills, knowledge, behaviours, attitude and impact.

Result: Wrap your narrative up with a quick summary of the result – what changed as a result of your actions? Focus here on what the key decision makers (here, or in another company) considered to be the worthwhile outcomes.

Learning not to say 'we' all the time makes a huge difference. It's interesting to video interviews and then run them back for the candidate, asking the question 'How much of the story was about you?'

Careers specialist Fiona Ward writes: 'When interviewing I have prompted candidates to speak about themselves, even to the extent of the direct question, "Tell me about your personal involvement", and they still say "we". Interestingly, when the same candidates receive feedback about how the interview went and are told this fact, they argue "But I told you what I did!"'

COMMERCIAL BREAK

Keep your stories tight and to the point. Think of the very tight storylines that are used in television advertising where there is a narrative – the scene is set quickly, and the point of the story is reached within 30 seconds or so. In an interview you may have a little longer, but the same principle applies. Each answer is like a TV ad for one particular competency – you have to get an idea across very quickly.

The art of storytelling is so important it gets special focus in Chapter 13, but it's worth emphasising here that there is a careful balance to be struck, especially when setting the scene in the opening part of your answer. Too much and the interviewer becomes frustrated; too little and your punch line falls flat because you haven't shown the size of the problem you solved.

Don't try to learn answers word for word, but prepare well enough so that you can address each competency with a brief, convincing narrative. Rehearsal, by the way, means speaking a story out loud at least three times until the material is safely embedded, awaiting your first competency-based question.

CHAPTER SEVENTEEN

How do I handle personal or oddball questions?

THIS CHAPTER LOOKS AT:

- What employers don't tell you about personality factors
- Sharpening up your self-awareness
- How every question is an assessment of personality
- New ideas regarding strengths and weaknesses
- Rolling with oddball questions

HOW FAR DO EMPLOYERS CONSIDER PERSONALITY?

In the past, interviews looked at intangible things like 'character', seeking evidence from your family background or schooling. Today, after a half century of attention to fairness in recruitment, employers are under pressure to seek only job-related evidence. However, CVs don't come to work, people do, and accurately predicting how someone will perform in a role is notoriously difficult. Under scrutiny on diversity issues, some employers only ask set questions about competencies, and never ask why you want the job (so tell them anyway – most candidates won't).

Employers don't like to admit to selecting on personality, but they do so every day, asking 'Can I work with this individual?' and 'Will this person fit into the team?' Often personality requirements are not documented, so two interviews exist simultaneously; the first ticking boxes on skills and competencies, while beneath the surface a second conversation is going on, driven by the interviewer's 'gut feel'. Career coach Beverley Grant says: 'In my experience eight or more out of ten candidates have not stopped to think about how important feelings are in an interview situation. Does anyone hire someone they don't like? Do you want to work for someone *you* don't like?'

Some employers test for specific personality traits, identifying factors such as extroversion, dominance, flexibility, robustness. These elements are then explored in behavioural questions looking at past situations, drawing out all the non-technical aspects of the job including attitude and team fit. Employers often believe they 'hire for attitude, train for aptitude' – most skills can be taught, but mindset is difficult to shift.

Personality factors are essential in a wide range of people-facing roles, and selectors will often be looking for the ability to build trust and win people over quickly. Leadership roles usually require an ability to influence others' behaviour and a degree of self-awareness of your impact on others. Other roles rely more heavily on your thinking style, your flexibility in changing circumstances, goal orientation, and the ability to think analytically, plan and manage projects. Some roles require emotional stability – working under pressure and in the face of criticism. You won't match all requirements – we are all a mix, with some factors stronger than others, and there is no 'right' balance. One accountant may be a strong analytical thinker not attuned to people, while another might shine at maintaining customer relationships.

KNOWING ENOUGH ABOUT YOUR PERSONAL STYLE

Successful managers are often relatively adaptable, capable of being directive or consultative, free thinking or rule-focused. Often the key thing is having enough self-awareness to know when to behave differently. Think about the way you react in different work situations. You're a stickler for detail, but can you also throw the rulebook out of the window from time to time? You may not be the life and soul of the party, but can you come out of your shell enough to make someone feel comfortable and welcome? Look at areas that a skilled interviewer will probe:

Three key areas for improved self-awareness

1   Think of occasions when you acted in ways which were an appropriately flexible response to circumstances (e.g. consciously letting someone else take the lead when you are naturally bossy).

2   What is your preferred working situation – in other words, the team and work context that brings out the best in you?

3   Reflect, honestly, on how you act under pressure (e.g. you usually consult people carefully but under time pressure you just get on with things).

One thing is clear, as Chapter 10 on first impressions reveals: being outgoing, personable and easy to talk to gets a warm response close to an early 'yes'. The good news is that you can adopt these behaviours. You probably do it already. Think about the last time you had to make a difficult phone call. You probably thought carefully about the words you would use, but also your tone of voice.

You don't need to become a party animal overnight, or suddenly super-confident. You will do well at interview if you remember how to be *you on a good day*.

QUESTIONS TO EXPECT

You may receive a person specification outlining personal characteristics as well as skills and knowledge. Even if this information is not explicit, you can generally work it out from the adjectives used (*consultative, diplomatic, organised, leader of change* ...). Think of times where you clearly demonstrated these personal qualities – what were you doing? You can also work out hidden personality requirements by thinking yourself into the job. What problems will this job solve? Who will you be working with and alongside? What pressures will there be on your performance?

HIDDEN MESSAGES

Even if you're answering questions about job knowledge or skill, you are subtly also answering questions about personality. Every answer you give contains a hidden message about your working style and your impact on others. For example, you might be describing your skills designing PowerPoint presentations, but in passing you mention your frustration at your boss who never briefs you properly and always drops tasks on you at the last moment. The interviewer's attention has shifted – you're broadcasting material on attitude and personality.

Watch out for the kind of discussion which is going to be a 'hot button' for personality evidence: following instructions; initiating and managing projects; innovation; teamworking; managing and motivating others; responding to criticism; working against deadlines; difficult colleagues or customers; working with people from backgrounds very different to your own.

REMEMBER THE DARK SIDE

A well-trained interviewer will probe for evidence of where things went wrong. Think about these stories in advance, because strong candidates talk about experiences where things didn't work out as they expected, or even times when things went completely wrong, but then show how they learned from the experience. A bit of humility helps, too – interviewers are naturally suspicious of candidates who got *everything* right. Remember that you're not building a fiction; you're trying to convey what you are like when you are working confidently and 'in the zone'. Often people are so worried about coming across as the wrong kind of person they try to hide evidence rather than showing a flexible working style.

HANDLING DIFFICULT PERSONAL QUESTIONS

Any question about your personal working style *feels* slightly invasive, particularly when it comes to your areas of vulnerability. Even people who are confident selling a product or service can find it hard to talk about themselves – selling yourself is a much riskier business, and 'no' feels much more personal. So, the reality is that both acceptable *and* unprofessional questions about personality are tricky to handle because we respond to them emotionally as well as intellectually.

The following provides a summary of the kinds of questions that are likely to come up, and some thoughts about how you deal with them:

- **Relationships** – can you establish them quickly? Can you build long-term relationships of trust? Employers like to hear that you can work with many different types of people to get things done – that when called for you can be polite, charming, diplomatic, motivating *and* stand your own ground when you need to.

- **Influence** – how effective are you at persuading others to think or act differently? Do you do this best verbally or in writing?

- **Decision making** – think about how you normally make

decisions. It's good to have examples of where you have done this cautiously, consultatively, taking account of facts and risks, but also times when you have grasped the nettle and trusted your judgement.

- **Resilience** – how long does it take you to bounce back after receiving tough criticism or a rejection? Your job search history will provide valuable clues.

- **Attention to detail** (how much detail is very job-specific) – are you a natural quality control person, or have you learned to delegate this to others?

- **Diplomacy** – how easy it for you to communicate effectively in a delicate situation? If this is not a strength, think about where you have sensibly farmed this out to someone with better 'radar'.

- **Management style** – if the position is a management role prepare short statements about your style as a manager. Employers usually like to hear that you get things done, on time and on target, without treading on too many toes.

- **Are you consultative?** Again, it's good to have examples of where you have taken consultation seriously, and times when you have recognised that you needed to act fast on limited information.

STRENGTHS AND WEAKNESSES

Most interviewers seem to find it important to ask about your strengths and weaknesses (perhaps because the world of business is steeped in SWOT analysis). My experience is that selection decisions are rarely made on these answers. To be safe don't talk about personal characteristics as strengths – talk about skills which closely match the job.

Some interviewees find it much easier to talk about their weaknesses than their strengths, so you may have to practise talking about what you have done well. When you do so, imagine you are talking about someone else – be accurate rather than over-egging or under-selling.

Interviewers usually tune out when candidates talk about strengths, then pay close attention to weaknesses in the hope that you will shoot yourself in the foot. So, don't introduce anything negative enough to raise concerns. It's often appropriate to talk about skills you want to develop further.

Classic advice suggests that you name weaknesses which are actually strengths (stickler for detail, workaholic, frustrated by lack of commitment in others) but unless you pitch this well it can sound clichéd. Career coach Ann Reynolds says: 'Tackle anything you fear might put the employer off selecting you, and tell them why this won't be a problem', so for example your approach might be to say, 'You might be concerned that I don't have enough big company experience, but in fact I have undertaken big consultancy projects with a range of blue chip organisations.'

Careers specialist Robin Rose's advice is not to use textbook answers, but refocus the question on your agenda: '"I've looked at the job description and I don't see any gaps." Admit any skill area where you may have to brush up and state, "I am confident I can do the job and in any event I'm a quick learner."'

CURVE BALL, LEFT FIELD, FANTASY AND DIFFICULT

Officially all selectors nod to the principle that questions should be fair and designed to see if you can do the job. In practice some of them come up with very strange questions – some interviewers believe that 'clever', quirky questions sort the sheep from the goats. The real reason, I suspect, is that interviewers get bored and want to spice things up.

There is no evidence to link quirky questions to evidence of job capability, but interviewers take a secret pride in inventing them: 'If you were a song, what song would you be? What's on your mantelpiece at home?' 'Are you a cat or a dog?' The Internet is full of examples.

Sometimes they are fantasy questions which may or may not be related to the job ('If you were a car, what model would you be?'), while others seek out ingenuity or lateral thinking ('If I put you in a sealed room with a phone that had no dial tone, how would you fix it?'). If you are going for a job requiring creative thinking, work out how you would tackle something like this. A small number of employers require candidates to undertake an even stranger mix of embarrassing tasks such as telling a joke or singing a song. They may just provide clues about candidates' ability to fit into certain cultures, but most times all that happens is that extroverts and actors get offers, not the people who can do the job.

Try to respond with good humour. Don't get flustered, because the only wrong answer is where you freeze like a rabbit in the headlights. Think of the very last item on *Question Time* – the witty, light response works best. If nothing else, say 'As I'll probably think of a great answer on the way home, can I email you later?' or 'You've got me there. I normally ask what animal in the jungle you'd be', and, whatever you do, smile.

Some questions are more appropriate than they seem. If higher reasoning is required, you might get the question put to one Cambridge University entrant: 'How do you know that California exists?' Some oddball questions are tests of lateral thinking and approximation; for example, 'How many light bulbs are in this building?' or 'How many packets of jelly would you need to fill St Paul's Cathedral?' (yes, there are rare candidates who can answer that by approximating cubic capacity). Remember that if you are asked to make calculations under pressure it is the thought process that counts, and an intelligent approximation rather than an exact figure is often acceptable.

CHAPTER EIGHTEEN

How do I get past sticky moments when things start to go wrong?

THIS CHAPTER LOOKS AT:

- The moments that throw you off your game
- Quick strategies for bouncing back
- Focusing on what's happening now, not what you've just done
- Taking the interviewer where you want to go

THAT AWKWARD MOMENT

Even the best-prepared interviews don't run exactly to order, and there are all kinds of questions that can throw you. Hopefully you won't be too thrown by predictable questions which you can handle with 'lifeboat answers' (see Chapter 12). There are, however, moments in an interview where you might think things are not going your way. This chapter outlines how this happens, and what you can do about it.

As a general principle, if you are thrown by a particular question don't try to answer when you are already on the back foot. Ask what underlies the question. So, for example, if you're asked 'Would you describe yourself as a perfectionist?' and you don't know how to pitch your answer, say something like 'Before answering that it would be helpful to know what level of detail is required in this job.'

YOU CAN'T THINK OF AN EXAMPLE

The most common area where people get stuck is when they are stumped by a question. If that happens, play for time: 'I'd like to match my experience as closely as possible to the job, so could you give me a little more insight about what this role requires?' If you can't think of an example from your working life, think about something taken from your life outside work. If you still can't think of an answer, say so rather than improvising badly. Then let it go; the moment has passed – if you keep thinking about what you were asked five minutes ago your attention will be in the wrong place. Next time prepare matching evidence more carefully.

YOU'RE STILL THINKING ABOUT WHAT YOU SAID 10 MINUTES AGO

Stuart McIntosh has reminded me of the lovely French expression – *l'esprit d'escalier* – the witty comeback you think of too late when you have left the room and are half way down the stairs. It is usually accompanied by regret ('if only I'd said …'), and a feeling that things would have gone better if you'd had the right words available.

This is potentially useful in hindsight to help you deliver better answers in future conversations. In the room itself this kind of thinking distracts you from the task in hand. It's like a Formula 1 driver always thinking about the last bend – your attention needs to be on the next piece of track.

Promise yourself that you won't be distracted into analysing your performance during the interview. Do that and you are not properly in the room, but watching yourself, critiquing your answers – plenty of time for that afterwards. Before you go in, say this aloud: 'During the interview I will focus only on the question I am answering.'

In the room focus only on what is going well, listen to what you are saying *right now*, rather than reflecting on what you said five minutes ago. Candidates who self-check all the time don't work hard enough on the relationship in the room, and are the ones who often say 'Can you repeat the question?'

YOU THINK OF A BETTER ANSWER LATER

As the interview progresses you might think of a better answer to an earlier question. Don't get too distracted by this – give your attention to the current question, and don't blurt out new information which is unrelated to the current topic of conversation. If you are convinced that a better answer might tick a box which the interviewer is uncertain about, make a quick judgement call. Will your answer score points, or get you into difficulty? Don't risk going back over old ground if your new answer won't survive probing. If you think it's important, ask permission towards the end: 'Earlier you asked me about X, I'd like to add ...'

YOU SAY NEGATIVE THINGS ABOUT YOURSELF

We have already established that negative information sticks. Sometimes an interviewer is still thinking about it when you have moved on to another topic. However, research undertaken by Daniel Cable and Virginia Kay, published by London Business School in 2011, indicates that candidates who were honest about their failings at interview did better in the long run than hired applicants who tended not to mention any negatives. Interestingly, those who revealed shortcomings were happier and more successful in their new jobs, felt a stronger commitment to their new employers, and received more favourable performance evaluations from supervisors after a year in their new jobs. This report concluded that the best recruitment decision would be to rule out candidates who disclosed no shortcomings.

Balance this against a 2010 feature in *Harvard Business Review* by Todd Rogers and Michael Norton which records that 'People who dodge questions artfully are liked and trusted more than people who respond to questions truthfully but with less polish.' Credibility is about how details are presented. The overall answer seems to be to combine both honesty and proficiency – *give polished answers, particularly about times where things went wrong.*

Career management specialist Zena Everett writes: 'Employers want to see that you are flexible, can learn and adapt. Acknowledge how you have learnt from your mistakes. When you describe past achievements, it's good to say what you would do differently next time: "At the end of the project when we reviewed how each stage had gone, we agreed that we should have stepped in as soon as we realised that the supplier wasn't communicating effectively and confronted their account manager earlier." That's not admitting a weakness, but demonstrating self-awareness, the ability to learn and to take constructive criticism. Also, that you have learnt on someone else's payroll so can hit the ground running when you join the new employer.'

YOU CRITICISE A PAST EMPLOYER

This flaw is generally best avoided, but if you have done it you have two strategies available. First, immediately say something positive as a counter-balance. This shows that you are capable of seeing the big picture, and seeing things from an organisational perspective. Second, when you are talking about another job or employer, make sure you are as positive as reasonably possible.

YOUR ANSWER DOESN'T SOUND AS GOOD AS IT DID WHEN YOU REHEARSED IT

This could, of course, be because you are under-rehearsed, but sometimes your well-prepared answer doesn't get the audience reaction you want. Interviewers are not always open in their reactions; you may be doing very well indeed, but the interviewer's professionalism means that little is being given away. Don't be put off: the same interviewers who appear detached at interview can be the most enthusiastic about your qualities afterwards.

However, a lack of response may reveal that you haven't put enough suspense in your story – you've described an achievement without showing the size of the challenge you faced. It might be because your story is still too long, and the interviewer is switching off part way through. In any event, don't change your strategy. Deciding half way through an interview to start cutting out material or improvising new stories is a bad idea.

Your background research needs to focus on the language that the employer is currently using to describe tasks, performance and success. Think also about the energy levels in your answers (see advice for introverts in Chapter 6). Don't just unpack your experience, learn how to sell it.

YOU'RE ASKED FOR BETTER EVIDENCE MORE CLOSELY RELATED TO THE JOB

Hopefully you will have done the right kind of matching when preparing, but it's always possible to misinterpret information (or the job documentation may not give away the employer's true wish list). Don't be put off by requests for more information on job fit – they are buying signals (you're close to the target) and it's much better to get the prompt now rather than negative feedback afterwards. If it's a competency-based interview you may have spoken about the right events, but not used the right language. If you are challenged to offer examples which are more closely related to an employer's needs, ask a question before diving in: 'Can you tell me a little more about what you're looking for?'

YOU'RE THROWN BY QUESTIONS ABOUT YOUR LONG-TERM CAREER PLANS

Sophie Rowan, author of *Brilliant Career Coach* (Prentice Hall, 2011), believes that employers ultimately buy into authenticity, which for her is much more than matching yourself to a set of competencies. It's about having a coherent story about your career as a whole – who you are, what you have to offer, where you see yourself in the future and how that fits the organisation and the role. Sophie's advice is to 'have a career purpose – choose your next career stage rather than your next job'. Authenticity, therefore, isn't just about sounding credible, it's about having a clear and valid reason for taking a particular role; the job on offer should sound like the best natural next step in your career path.

Zena Everett draws on her hiring experience: 'Recruiters want to see that candidates have demonstrated control and ownership of their career path and that their reasons for wanting to join the organisation are based on a clear career strategy. Their career objectives should dovetail with the organisation's strategic objectives and the objectives of the role.'

A classic question that could put you on the back foot is 'Where do you want to be in five years' time?' Clichéd answers usually involve arrogance or over-optimism. No organisation can really predict what its key players will be doing this far ahead, so talk about personal development rather than ambition. A good strategy is to shorten the timeframe: 'I don't know where I'll be in five years, but within a year, I hope to win several large accounts.'

YOUR INITIAL ANSWER NEEDED A SECOND LINE OF DEFENCE

Chapter 16 on probing questions outlined the difference between first level questions which look for surface detail, and second and third level questions which probe detail or credibility. Anticipate difficult areas by building lines of defence around issues that you know will be probed. So, for example, you might have left your last job because you were under-employed. Your first line of defence is simplicity, and a short but positive answer: 'I moved on because I wanted more of a challenge.'

Hold your second line of defence for where an interviewer says 'I'd like to know a bit more about that ...' Here you will give a more developed but equally balanced answer: 'I had learned as much as I could in the job and my employer was reluctant to expand the job any further, so I decided it was time to look for something which would stretch me, and this job ...'. Taking your answer from your past (your experience) to the present (the job under discussion) is always a good move.

THE INTERVIEWER SEEMS TO DISAPPROVE OF YOUR ANSWER

While interviewers often give little away, early signals that you are not delivering the right kind of material are helpful indications that you need to change strategy. Don't make this a challenge ('I don't seem to be giving you what you're looking for' or 'You're not asking about my experience of X ...'). If in doubt, ask – seek a recap of what the interviewer is looking for, or ask 'Would it be helpful if I talked about ...?'

THE INTERVIEWER LOOKS BORED

If interviewers see a lot of people, they get bored, sometimes quite easily. That's why it's important to be memorable, and to be memorable you need to be interesting. Spinning tales rather than dumping information makes all the difference – strong candidates are often very entertaining to listen to. It's difficult to suddenly switch this on in the room but energised language gets the interviewer's attention as much as energised behaviour – consciously use words like 'exciting', 'success', 'challenge' or 'buzz', or try saying 'There's quite a good story behind this one …'

An interviewer has got to enjoy you. Experienced recruiter Melanie Moore says: 'I interview 5–10 people a week and it is the ones that are honest, interesting, friendly and open that I enjoy the most. I have to "sell" these candidates to companies and so I need to trust what they say and enjoy meeting them.'

YOU DON'T GET TO THE TOPICS YOU FIND IT EASY TO TALK ABOUT

I am indebted to my colleague Kate Howlett for this one. Remember the hot and cold game you played as a child? Shouting 'hotter' when someone got close to the hidden object? Play the same game in interviews. Give short answers to negative questions, and longer answers to positive questions, so you control the amount of time given to positive information. It's your job to take the interview to a 'hot' place every time you can.

CHAPTER NINETEEN

I get interviews, but not job offers ...

THIS CHAPTER LOOKS AT:

- The real reasons why jobs are not offered
- Understanding what's actually about you, and what isn't
- Inner ring statistics
- Re-energising yourself with small changes

IT'S A NO, THEN

It's a genuinely downbeat experience. You're up for a job that you are excited about and you feel well equipped to undertake. You've done your homework, prepared successfully for the interviewer's most likely questions, and pitched in some good answers. Sure, there is always something extra you could have done, but you had a pretty convincing interview. And yet you get the same rejection letter as someone who did no homework and did all the wrong things: *Thank you so much for your application. Unfortunately ...*

BEGIN WITH WHAT IS WORKING

Any 'no' which is about you, personally, has the potential to knock you back, and some people find that rejection has a knock-on effect on confidence.

Reflect on what you said, and also why you might have failed to get the right evidence across at interview, but don't become entirely wrapped up in the things that didn't go well. Rethinking an interview answer after the event is natural and may help you to phrase things better next time. However, it's possible to get totally bogged down in the negative aspects, constantly reliving past interviews, especially as the uncomfortable moments are the ones you will remember most. Sit down with a good friend or a career coach and go through the interview, point by point. Try to remember the *exact words* of both the questions and your answers. Agree the things that worked. Perhaps you gave thoughtful answers and strong evidence, perhaps a story went well and got you past a difficult issue. Zero in on what went well, because that's where your next interview begins – you will always achieve more by building on success rather than failure.

Think about learning to drive. The first few times at the wheel you will make mistakes, forget which is the windscreen wipers and which the indicators, time things wrong, stall at the junction – loss of dignity is lesson number one. However, you will never learn to be a better driver by beating yourself up. You get better by observing the times you get things right and saying 'That's how it works, I'll remember that', or 'What can I do to stop repeating that mistake?'

You learn in a variety of ways, including experiment. Sometimes you get a breakthrough by doing things completely differently and sometimes by thinking about what you do very differently. There are many ways forward, even if you think you're not making any progress at all – you just need the right feedback, practice, or a new way of thinking.

THEY SEEM DISAPPOINTED WHEN IT'S ME TURNING UP

Ever had that experience? The person greeting you looks slightly confused, and probably looks you up and down. You're not what they expected. This is good news in one way – your CV, covering letter and initial phone conversations have worked well enough to get you short listed. However, your first impression is not what you should be aiming for (perhaps on paper you are 'top saleswoman' but at interview you come across as 'harassed mother of three').

Again, distinguish between gut feel and genuine feedback as it's easy to jump at shadows and begin to build a whole set of theories about how people react. However, if you get the same feeling on several occasions, corroborated by feedback from those who know you well, you are probably sending out conflicting messages – one on paper and one in person.

THE REAL REASONS YOU MIGHT NOT GET A JOB OFFER

Understand the difference between results and feedback. There are all kinds of things going on under the bonnet in staff selection.

Reasons to do with you

- You are a poor match for the role. This may sound obvious, but see the paragraph below on 'inner ring statistics'. If it was a long shot, it remains a long shot even if you have got to the interview.

- You failed to get across the minimum key messages needed to take you to the next round. This is a failure of preparation: you don't need to focus on everything, just the messages that count.

- You broadcast on the wrong wavelength at interview. This could be about the way you speak, dress or behave. Feedback in this area may help generally, or may simply reflect why your approach didn't work on one occasion.

- You showed lack of interest in the job. This could be about preparation, looking in depth at the organisation, but could equally be about enthusiasm. Remember that employers buy into energy before they buy into hard facts.

- You talked yourself out of the job. The job was a good match, you were a strong candidate, but your interview technique let you down. That's useful feedback, because it shows you are getting close to your target role but need to do some work.

- You communicated superiority and frustration because the interview requires you to go through a process you see as pointless – surely it's obvious you can do the job?

- You take yourself far too seriously, perhaps believing that your personality or background are 'complex'. You may feel you're a mystery wrapped inside an enigma, but to an interviewer you may sound like someone who finds it difficult to adapt.

Reasons (largely) outside your control

- The chemistry was wrong. While you have some responsibility for warmth of response in the room, some people's interactions just don't work. If it felt uncomfortable for you *and* the interviewer, that may be a sign that you are not a good fit for the organisational culture.

- Employers regularly make decisions which are highly subjective, for example based on non-verbal behaviours, personal prejudices or pure instinct. There is even evidence to suggest some interviewers are subtly influenced by physical attractiveness, believing that attractive people are more socially competent. Some interviewers are highly influenced by quality of voice or regional accents.

- Job descriptions are often far from accurate. You may be trying to match yourself against something which is a long way from the real job, which is why you need to undertake research beyond basic job information.

- Recruitment is often inaccurate. Employers don't always know exactly what they are looking for or how to spot it.

- Recruitment is a fluid process. Some organisations re-invent the role half way through once they have seen some candidates.

- Recruitment occasionally goes off the rails. Employers suffer hiring freezes, encounter delays, or change their minds about if, when or how a job will be filled. Sometimes a senior manager decides that the job needs filling in a different way.

- Your prospects may be shaped by the last person who did the job. If there is a question about whether an organisation really wants an external, dynamic candidate and the last person they appointed was exactly that but only stayed three months, you are tarred with the same brush.

- The job may already have someone's name on it. Don't be depressed by this fact – it could be a hiring pattern that one day works in your favour. However, if the job is already earmarked for a favoured person, internal or external, your chances of being anything more than interview fodder were always very slim.

- The market is tight, and the employer is overwhelmed with top-notch candidates. You might make an impression, but in a tough field it's difficult to be the number one choice. However, getting shortlisted does show that your strategy is working.

INNER RING STATISTICS

I am indebted to advice from my colleague Stuart McIntosh. We all love statistics and hit rates, he suggests, and it is easy to proudly count up rejection letters or applications that failed. We need to be careful about the way we count 'failures'. Reviewing your job search effectiveness it's easy to say, for example, 'I applied for fifty jobs, got four interviews, and only got to second interview once; no job offers.'

That might sound like a ratio of 50 to 1, but you're allowing junk statistics to drive an emotional response: *my CV isn't working ... I don't interview well ... I'd better lower my sights ...* That voice in your head that says *none of this is working* can easily persuade you to rewrite your CV or radically adjust your interview technique, but if you count every rejection as a failure you will repeatedly make random adjustments without necessarily improving anything.

See Chapter 20 for ways of discerning the difference between random feedback and solid information. As this chapter shows, there are all kinds of arbitrary reasons why you might not get a job offer, and *most of them have nothing to do with you.*

Look dispassionately at your job search (enlist help if you find it hard to be objective). Divide your applications into the four categories in your Job Application Dartboard:

Job Application Dartboard

● **Inner ring** – jobs close to or within the bull's eye of your dartboard. In other words, jobs you are able to do and would be interested in doing.

FIGURE 19.1 *Job Application Dartboard*

- **Outer ring** – jobs some way off the bull's eye. You might be able to do the job but you are not sure if it's really you, and other people might have more obviously appropriate skill sets.

- **Holes in the wallpaper** – shots that didn't even hit the dartboard – jobs that you have little interest in or jobs for which you have little if any matching experience.

- **Floor shots** – jobs that you definitely didn't want but you applied for them 'for the experience'. A long way off target, and probably not good for your confidence anyway (see Chapter 6 on applying for jobs for 'practice').

Look again at your inner ring job applications. How many of them have you actually managed to identify? If not many, rethink your job search strategy, not your interview technique. You just aren't getting in front of the right people. If you find that you have made a genuinely large number of inner ring job applications (this is rare – most people shoot all round the dartboard) and you are getting the same results, that's feedback. You may be aiming at the wrong target, or (more probably) you need to fine-tune your technique.

What about the rest of the dartboard? These will always be long shots. Do continue to apply for outer ring jobs, but don't count them or wallpaper or floor shots in your statistics. They are your wild throws, and any feedback you get from those interview experiences is not much help. It will generally be a variant on 'we had many candidates who were a better match for the role', and no surprise at all.

Job applications as a game of darts? It's a pretty good analogy. Clients often have a tight set of requirements: job type, salary, nice people and a good location. If their initial job search doesn't get results they usually introduce phrases like 'lowering my sights' or 'being more realistic'. The question I put to them is this: *If you're not getting close to the bull's eye, do you want a bigger dartboard, or do want to learn to aim better?*

REPEATED, CONSISTENT REJECTION

If you really are doing well at interviews (how do you judge that?) but not getting the job, what can you do about it? Do try to get valid feedback, as Chapter 20 suggests. Assuming that you are not ignoring the obvious (e.g. you lack a significant piece of paper, yawn through every interview, or always say 'really, I'm looking for a quiet life'), the answer may be difficult to hear. Be clear – we are only talking about repeated rejection for *inner ring* jobs as defined above. It would be nice to simply write this all off as one of the mysteries of the universe, but any experienced recruiter will give you a straight answer to this puzzle.

In the absence of alternative hard evidence, what remains is the distinct possibility that you are just not getting the relationship right in the room. As you realise, getting this right every time is hard work (see in particular Chapter 17 on personality-based questions) but if you repeatedly fail to get the job because you're told you don't demonstrate sufficient 'fit', you need to look at what you can change. With repeated rejections at the final stage, an experienced career coach would put money on the reason falling within these top six:

1 first impressions;

2 chemistry;

3 appearing personable;

4 body language;

5 saying too much;

6 underplaying your achievements.

You may have problem areas outside this list, but it's unlikely.

CHAPTER TWENTY

I am confused by interview feedback

THIS CHAPTER LOOKS AT:

- The effects of good, indifferent and meaningless feedback
- Knowing what is feedback and what isn't
- Real feedback that has helped candidates transform their performance
- When and how to ask

FEEDBACK – WHAT FEEDBACK?

This chapter starts with an optimistic assumption – that you will get some kind of feedback after an interview. In fact too often candidates don't get objective and helpful feedback at any stage in the interview process – whether the process had a positive result or not.

Job searchers need to get to grasp an important reality: recruiters and interviewers are not officially in the advice business. Thankfully we can all point to noble exceptions to the rule – individuals who have provided us with encouragement as well as valuable tips – but the rule still holds. A decision maker is interested in filling a role, not counselling you through the process of job change.

HOW MUCH FEEDBACK SHOULD YOU EXPECT?

You have no automatic right to feedback. An employer is entitled to make a decision – there is no legal requirement even to inform candidates that they have been rejected. Believing that feedback after an interview is something you are 'owed' is as misguided as complaining about the process or challenging the result. These behaviours simply put you into the opposition camp.

You should ask for feedback (but only if you know how to interpret it, build on it, and not be confused by it, which is why this chapter exists); however, you should not expect to receive it as a right or as a standard stage in the recruitment process.

A vast amount of information masquerades as feedback. You will be told all kinds of things about what an interviewer likes or dislikes. Some of this is quite simply a matter of interviewer prejudice (brown shoes in the city, wearing scent, taking gap years …), some of it strong opinion (for example, about how many pages your CV should contain, or whether you should mention your interests outside work). There are probably as many opinions out there as interviewing styles.

IS IT WORTH ASKING FOR FEEDBACK?

I have been tempted in public to give a definitive 'no' to this question, and the jury is still out. So much feedback is either bland or misleading, and often sends candidates on a wild goose chase.

Be clear – sometimes there are hard and fast reasons why you don't get a job (you might lack management experience or language skills, for example), but at the final selection stage such clear-cut reasons are unusual. It is rare that an interviewer gives you a useful breakdown of the strengths and weaknesses of your performance; more frequently you hear something bland but vaguely troubling.

For example, an interviewer says 'your examples were a

little long'. So you adjust your strategy for all future interviews, chopping out good information and not telling the full story. Perhaps the interview feedback was 'some of your evidence wasn't recent enough', so you start to drop good evidence. You might hear 'you don't have enough leadership experience', and you believe you're not a leader. Feedback which is explicitly about your personality knocks your confidence even more.

A great deal of feedback is code for 'we chose someone else, get over it' or even 'we're not sure, so don't ask'. Feedback easily slides into rejection: you don't feel good about it, and you haven't learned anything either. The danger is that next you adjust your behaviours, hoping for a different result. This is not actually a strategy, just a hope that the dice will fall differently next time.

Don't tinker with your interview approach unless you get *genuine feedback you can do something about*. This is not, by the way, a free ride for those who don't feel there is any room for improvement in their interview skills; that's the deafness of egotism talking – we all need to learn and adapt.

THE REAL DEAL

What does good feedback look like? It is a set of responses that prompts you to improve the way you do things. Valid feedback will tell you how your practised performance actually works – there's a difference between encouragement from a kindly driving instructor and cold facts from your examiner.

Here are some examples of critical feedback that some of my clients have been given that helped them to quickly get to a winning interview performance:

- Speaking too much so that the interviewer couldn't hear the right evidence or get all the questions in.

- Appearing too reserved and not sounding excited by the role.

- Being inappropriately assertive and 'in your face'.

- Underplaying strengths and achievements.

- Failing to translate experience into language the interviewer got excited by.

- Not covering all the bases in terms of the interviewer's short list.

- Being floored by personal or quirky questions.

- Failing to read the room and establish some kind of relationship with everyone present.

- Failure to demonstrate an understanding of the needs and problems which cause the job to exist.

- Not making sense of your career to date.

- Failing to get primary messages across.

WHY BOTHER WITH FEEDBACK AT ALL?

Some people are gifted at seeing themselves the way others see them, some less so. Most of us have blind spots – there are things you do well that you don't see (so can't build on them) and things you do badly that you are blind to (and therefore can't deal with them). Interestingly, it takes only a small amount of live performance feedback to address these issues. The mistake candidates make is to ask employers to do this.

You only get feedback, in reality and on a good day, on about 10 per cent of your performance. Therefore even assuming every employer is insightful and generous enough to deliver, it could still take 10 or more interviews to get anything like the complete picture. Far more effective and economical, surely, to get near-complete feedback on one occasion which is unconnected to a real job decision.

Some things you can address through practice interviews. Perhaps you use the same expression too much. You might 'um' and 'er', or take too long to think of an answer (unprepared it can take people 20–30 seconds to come up with a reasonable answer to a high level question). You might speak too quietly or say things in an undertone at the end of an answer. You might lose track of the question. All this is for the practice zone. Don't use a real job interview to discover the basics, because it's a wasted opportunity.

Feedback can sometimes show you that you did the wrong kind of research, or misunderstood what the organisation was looking for – all good learning points. However, most times you can be a good judge of how well prepared you were – score yourself out of 10 on your preparation for every interview, and then work out what you need to do to improve that score by one point. You can't go from 2 out of 10 to full marks overnight, but you would be surprised how easily a quick fix will get you to something more like 7 out of 10. Understand the difference between perfect and 'good enough'.

Of the hundreds of individuals I have coached through job interviews, even the most confident has improved in both effectiveness and confidence just by answering real, penetrating questions in a rehearsal interview. It needs to be demanding, it needs to feel real, and it needs to be conducted by someone who has experience of putting real questions to real candidates. You can even write the questions for them, but it is vital that you answer them with the same voice and the same seriousness that you would do 'live'. If the answer is too long, too woolly, or doesn't come out right, do it again. Don't accept bland encouragement – if the answer was good, find out why. Ask for your evidence to be tested. Invite tough questions on the topics you don't want to talk about. Very little in an interview should be improvised, but what you say should *sound* lively and spontaneous.

THE BEST WAY TO ASK FOR FEEDBACK

Organisations, and the interviewers representing them, do not like anything which sounds like a challenge to a hiring decision. So any question that sounds like 'Why wasn't I selected?' is a complete no-go. Employers are worried about litigation, so will always answer a challenge with some variant of this standard paragraph: *We were delighted to meet you at interview. There was a very strong field of applicants and we were able to offer the role to someone who more closely met our requirements.* What do you learn from that? Nothing. It does not mean that you didn't meet the selection criteria or that you had some kind of gap in your evidence. It simply tells you that someone else got the job.

We have already agreed that interview feedback is a bonus, not a right. So, if you get it, listen carefully, take notes, and then reflect on what you have heard. However, do ask the right question. The question 'What did I do wrong?' or 'What were my weaknesses at interview?' still sound to an employer like 'Why didn't you give me the job?' A far better approach is 'I enjoyed the interview and I'm delighted you found the right candidate. It would really help me in future interviews if you could give me one or two tips about my interview perfor- mance. What did I do well? What could I have done better?' Starting with a positive makes it easier for the interviewer, and may even boost your confidence. You are also getting the interviewer to think about actual behaviours and performance – what you actually did, not what they liked or disliked about you. Focusing on future interviews means that your question has nothing to do with this particular role.

SECOND INTERVIEW

You may get feedback between a first and second interview – 'We enjoyed meeting you and we'd like to continue the conversation.' Any invitation to a second interview is always an opportunity to find out what has worked so far. A question along the lines of 'I'd be interested to know what aspects of my experience have taken me to the next stage' is always helpful, quickly followed by 'It would help my preparation to know where you have any concerns or where I should supply more details.'

FEEDBACK VS. DATA

When you are thinking over feedback you have received, do learn to distinguish between facts and 'spin'. We've already discussed the difference between feedback which is specific (this job, this organisation) and generic (all job applications, all future interviews).

Do remember that interviewers, particularly those working for intermediaries (recruitment agencies) often hold strong opinions about things like CV format, interview dress code, interview style, questions you should always or never ask, and so on. Some of this is useful, some of it is entirely context-driven. The rule here is simple – if you get similar feedback from several sources (for example, 'you are not communicating your skills in the right language for our sector'), that's tangible feedback you can work with.

Finally, and please print this in large letters and stick it inside the front cover of your job application file:

REJECTION IS NOT FEEDBACK

Rejection is just rejection, and a great deal of feedback is just noise. Unless, that is, it's consistent and repeated (Chapter 19 shows you the dangers of interpreting your misses on the Job Application Dartboard, and Chapter 6 offers warnings about attending interviews 'just for practice').

There are many, many reasons why you might not get short listed for a role, and (particularly if this happens before the job interview stage) most reasons are much more about the arbitrariness of the process than they are about your application. It's tempting to put yourself centre stage, but believe me, most reasons for rejection *are not about you.*

So don't feel you always need to rewrite your CV, learn new interview answers, or even give up, because you are experiencing a feeling, not getting feedback. In fact, if you get a 'no', don't start adjusting your CV or trashing your interview skills. Go and do something entirely different which is not related to job seeking – cycle up a hill, go to a movie, go shopping – do whatever you normally do to feel good about life, and review your results later when you have a clearer, cooler mind.

CHAPTER TWENTY-ONE

My interview is tomorrow!

THIS CHAPTER LOOKS AT:

- Your roadmap for this book if you are preparing at the last minute
- Qualifying yourself for the job
- Beginnings and endings
- A reminder of what an employer is looking for
- Follow-up strategies

WHAT CAN I DO IN 24 HOURS?

Actually, 24 hours is just about enough time to prepare for an interview. If you've turned to this chapter it's probably because you are preparing the night before the interview in just a couple of hours, and feeling rather stressed about it. It's time to review the essentials.

The biggest antidote to interview stress is the right kind of preparation. This does *not* mean researching or worrying all night and not getting any sleep, going over your answers again and again, or anticipating worst-case scenarios. It means doing enough preparation, and then trusting in what you know. Your brain has far more capacity for recall under pressure than you imagine – do your preparation, rehearse your key answers two or three times, and then leave it alone. If all you do is follow this chapter, you may well have done more preparation than the average candidate, and good enough is a reasonable point to stop.

You might want to put all your energy into what you will say; save some attention for how your message will come across. Don't just lay out your interview clothes for the morning, put them on, and make sure they are well-pressed and comfortable. Stand in front of a mirror, and close your eyes. Remember a time you did really well at work, and felt on top of the world. Stand square with your shoulders back, and revel in that moment. Now open your eyes and see the person you hope an interviewer will see as you walk in through the door.

CRASH PREPARATION

You might be tempted to rely on luck. Think again – that's another excuse for not doing what you can do in the time available; lucky candidates are the ones who bring the right message into the room. Do what research you can. If time is really tight, look at the employer's website and find **one** interesting thing you can say about the organisation when you are greeted, and **two** pieces of information that you might introduce during the interview as comments or questions. Get your documents straight, and put them into a folder which should be the only thing you take into the interview room.

Next, spend some time reviewing the employer's shopping list. Use the 'One-sheet matching' exercise in Chapter 7 (on page 60) to predict questions, and start to line up your corresponding evidence.

Have a look at Chapter 13 on stories – you'll see how storytelling is a powerful way to get your best material across in a punchy, memorable package. The night before an interview you may not be able to rehearse a fund of stories, so go for half a dozen good ones – look at the things you believe to be the big ticket items and play the '**six for six**' game (page 32 in Chapter 4).

Sharpen up your key messages. What are your top skills? What gives you energy in a job? Plan in advance to be explicit about how you can add to the job. 'Armed with this information you can make positive suggestions about the future of the role in discussion', writes career coach Jim Currie. 'In the final analysis the interviewer is going to be more convinced by someone who understands his problems and how they can be solved than having to deduce it from what that interviewee has done in different jobs.'

One way or another you will be asked why you fit the job. Even if you get a broad opener like 'tell me about yourself', use this as an opportunity to sell yourself against four or five top skill areas. Be ready to wrap the interview up with some clear reasons about why you should be hired. This is not the kind of self-aggrandising statement you hear on *The Apprentice* – that empty language doesn't work here. A simple conversation where you match yourself point-for-point against the employer's checklist will instantly lift your interview. An employer who hears that you understand the job – and you are enthusiastic to solve its problems – will pay you close attention.

Don't think of an interview as a one-way conversation. Sophie Rowan of Pinpoint in Dublin says: 'Do what you can to equalise the balance of power in an interview by seeing yourself on equal terms – you're there to solve problems and contribute to needs.'

Finally, don't neglect to prepare yourself personally (Chapter 6 will help), and focus on approaching the interview not only with a positive attitude but also with the right energy – pay particular attention to your communication style whether you are naturally quiet and under-sell yourself or more gregarious and loud. Make sure your style is tempered to match that of the interviewer.

CHANGE A LITTLE, CHANGE A LOT

Perhaps your last interview didn't go as well as it could have? Most times, particularly after just one or two interviews, small changes make a big difference. Just slowing down and learning to be very still (see Chapter 5) helps with pre-match nerves. Learning and practising some robust '**lifeboat answers**' (Chapter 12) can make an overnight difference to the way you handle difficult questions.

However, if you keep putting in the same interview performance and get repeated knock-backs, something about *you* is getting in the way. If it's a question of verbal tics, self-criticism or projected attitude problems – what can you actually do the night before the interview? Three things: slow down, say less, and say *mainly the things you have prepared to say*. Know what you are going to say *before* your brain puts your tongue in gear.

BEGINNINGS AND ENDINGS

Since the opening and close of the interview are remembered most clearly, work hard on both, including your final questions and your final thank you.

Practise opening lines – if you fluff them, it will feed the part of your brain trying to persuade you that you don't interview well. Boost your confidence by arming yourself with small talk about the locality, organisation, or big news events that are affecting this employer. As Chapter 10 on **first impressions** reveals, interviewers make swift judgements in the opening moments, so be as easy to get on with as you can, rather than sitting there looking defensive or passively waiting for the first question. Tick the first box on the interviewer's checklist by saying something relaxed and interesting. Do the same with reception staff – they are often asked what they think of candidates.

Career coach Kathryn Jackson advises: 'Treat each

interview as though it has three parts – and you have to make a great impression at each stage; the introduction (have a great handshake, big smile, excellent eye contact), the middle (prepare your answers to questions that will come up), the end (finish on a really strong note, check that you've asked when you can expect to hear an outcome from the interview, ask for the job, thank your interviewer for their time). Asking for the job is something that I would always recommend at the end of an interview – not down on one knee grovelling, but ensuring that you make it clear the interview has impressed you, helped you to realise that you'd really like a role in the company and ask what the next steps are.'

MANAGING YOUR AIRTIME

On the morning news every day you will hear key figures from public life being interviewed. Some of them are easily thrown off track by the questions; the ones with media training stick solidly to what they have to say. They have been advised that the busy morning public will probably absorb little more than two or three pieces of information. No matter what questions are asked, a savvy interviewee will get two, three or four strong points across. The questions just provide an opportunity: the airtime is being used to convey a few, predetermined messages.

You can use the same technique. What three things would you like the interviewer to remember about you? These points might be issues that won't naturally come up (for example, you might want to draw out your valuable cross-sector experience). If you haven't found the opportunity during the interview, make your points at the end. Write these points down in advance, and practise short, clear summaries.

I have seen this technique applied many times in practice. Candidates go into interviews armed with three well-rehearsed positive messages, and afterwards if interviewers are asked to summarise what they have heard, the three messages are nearly

always repeated, and remembered. Rather than random information, you can attempt to plant the ideas and phrases you
would like to travel without you. What kind of things need to
be in these summary messages? Examples will include:

● Something that makes sense of an unusual background
  (your qualifications, background, career path).

● A strap-line statement which sums you up ('I like pushing
  people hard to help them get results they are proud of').

● Something which links two or more pieces of information
  in your CV ('My media studies background has given me
  a creative edge in the world of retail').

● Something which gets you past a difficult issue ('I decided
  to stop studying my A levels for a reason – to take up a
  dream job offer').

● A unique selling point ('You'll get plenty of people with
  my experience, but I believe my insights into the world of
  fashion give me a different perspective').

● (Particularly if you are not asked) one thing you will add
  to the job within the first 90 days (see Chapter 9).

● At least one thing about why you match the role ('The
  reason I'd be really excited to do this job …').

FINAL OVERVIEW

Jo Bond, who is CEO & Group Chair of Vistage International,
and a leadership and development coach, has developed a
great overview that I think you'll find a useful pre-interview
checklist:

What employers do and don't want to see (and hear) in job interviews

EMPLOYERS WANT TO SEE OR HEAR:

- Candidates who project energy and enthusiasm – have you got the get-up-and-go to perform the role in a high-performing way? Think about the interviewers as your target audience – you are marketing yourself to them. Put yourself in their shoes and think what you would want to see and hear.

- Evidence-based answers to questions – examples of real achievements that highlight the challenges that were overcome. Use metrics as much as possible, e.g. how much did revenue increase, costs decrease, client satisfaction improve, etc.

- Succinct responses to questions – avoid waffling on to fill in the pauses and gaps. Practise getting comfortable with silence in interviews. Say what you need to say then stop!

- A handful of carefully considered questions that demonstrate a real interest in the organisation and show you've prepared for the interview by researching in advance.

EMPLOYERS DON'T WANT TO SEE OR HEAR:

- Negative comments about your previous or current organisation/manager/co-workers.

- Why you don't have 100 per cent of all the desirable points in the advert – focus on what you have, your

▶

strengths and positive attributes. Employers are often
sceptical of those who score full marks on all the
desirables – they doubt those applicants will find the
job demanding enough.

- Salary negotiation points – that comes later: your
  greatest power is later when they declare that they
  want you. Avoid talking salary specifics.

Jo Bond, Vistage International

FOLLOW UP

At interview try to get clear answers about what happens next,
but don't panic if you don't hear anything. There are still one
or two things you can do.

'Is the interview over when it's finished?' asks career coach
Malcolm Watt. 'No. As soon as possible send a thank-you and
follow-up letter, expressing your keen interest in the company
and the job and asking when you might hear the result of the
interview if you haven't been told when to expect it during your
conversation.' Recruiter Graeme Dixon has a similar view: 'At
the end of the interview it is essential to thank them for their
time and ask if they have any concerns why they would not
progress their application. After the interview send a letter of
thanks with a couple of lines why you are suitable. Virtually
100 per cent of candidates do not do this and it differentiates
them from the competition.'

STEPPING FORWARD

Doing well at interviews isn't just about getting a job, it's about
doing better at work and getting more out of your career. The
skills you are learning while you prepare for the interview will

also make a big difference to so many other things you do in work – communicating, influencing, building relationships quickly, getting your point across in a memorable and engaging manner, persuading others to make a decision in your favour. These are the building blocks of a well-managed career.

So, even if you have just dipped into the chapters that addressed your immediate problems, you've taken some important steps forward. Keep learning, experimenting and improving – then when you walk into your next interview you'll find that luck walks into the room with you.

Index